PRACTICE STANDARD FOR PROJECT ESTIMATING – SECOND EDITION

Library of Congress Cataloging-in-Publication Data

Names: Project Management Institute, issuing body.
Title: Practice standard for project estimating / Project Management
    Institute.
Description: Second edition. | Newtown Square, Pennslyvania : Project
    Management Institute, Inc., [2019] | Includes bibliographical references
    and index. | Summary: "Developed within the framework of A Guide to the
    Project Management Body of Knowledge (PMBOK® Guide) - Sixth Edition and
    other PMI standards, the Practice Standard for Project Estimating -
    Second Edition focuses on providing models for the project management
    profession in both plan-driven and change-driven adaptive (agile) life
    cycles. This practice standard describes the aspects of project
    estimating that are recognized as good practice on most projects most of
    the time and that are widely recognized and consistently applied"--
    Provided by publisher.
Identifiers: LCCN 2019050072 (print) | LCCN 2019050073 (ebook) | ISBN
    9781628256420 (paperback) | ISBN 9781628256437 (epub) | ISBN
    9781628256444 (kindle edition) | ISBN 9781628256451 (adobe pdf)
Subjects: LCSH: Project management--Estimates. | Project
    management--Standards. | Cost control.
Classification: LCC HD69.P75 P652 2019 (print) | LCC HD69.P75 (ebook) |
    DDC 658.15/54--dc22
LC record available at https://lccn.loc.gov/2019050072
LC ebook record available at https://lccn.loc.gov/2019050073

ISBN: 978-1-62825-642-0

Published by:
    Project Management Institute, Inc.
    14 Campus Boulevard
    Newtown Square, Pennsylvania 19073-3299 USA
    Phone: +610-356-4600
    Fax: +610-356-4647
    Email: customercare@pmi.org
    Internet: www.PMI.org

To place a Trade Order or for pricing information, please contact Independent Publishers Group:
    Independent Publishers Group
    Order Department
    814 North Franklin Street
    Chicago, IL 60610 USA
    Phone: +1 800-888-4741
    Fax: +1 312-337-5985
    Email: orders@ipgbook.com (For orders only)

For all other inquiries, please contact the PMI Book Service Center.
    PMI Book Service Center
    P.O. Box 932683, Atlanta, GA 31193-2683 USA
    Phone: 1-866-276-4764 (within the U.S. or Canada) or +1-770-280-4129 (globally)
    Fax: +1-770-280-4113
    Email: info@bookorders.pmi.org

10 9 8 7 6 5 4 3 2 1

NOTICE

The Project Management Institute, Inc. (PMI) standards and guideline publications, of which the document contained herein is one, are developed through a voluntary consensus standards development process. This process brings together volunteers and/or seeks out the views of persons who have an interest in the topic covered by this publication. While PMI administers the process and establishes rules to promote fairness in the development of consensus, it does not write the document and it does not independently test, evaluate, or verify the accuracy or completeness of any information or the soundness of any judgments contained in its standards and guideline publications.

PMI disclaims liability for any personal injury, property or other damages of any nature whatsoever, whether special, indirect, consequential or compensatory, directly or indirectly resulting from the publication, use of application, or reliance on this document. PMI disclaims and makes no guaranty or warranty, expressed or implied, as to the accuracy or completeness of any information published herein, and disclaims and makes no warranty that the information in this document will fulfill any of your particular purposes or needs. PMI does not undertake to guarantee the performance of any individual manufacturer or seller's products or services by virtue of this standard or guide.

In publishing and making this document available, PMI is not undertaking to render professional or other services for or on behalf of any person or entity, nor is PMI undertaking to perform any duty owed by any person or entity to someone else. Anyone using this document should rely on his or her own independent judgment or, as appropriate, seek the advice of a competent professional in determining the exercise of reasonable care in any given circumstances. Information and other standards on the topic covered by this publication may be available from other sources, which the user may wish to consult for additional views or information not covered by this publication.

PMI has no power, nor does it undertake to police or enforce compliance with the contents of this document. PMI does not certify, test, or inspect products, designs, or installations for safety or health purposes. Any certification or other statement of compliance with any health or safety-related information in this document shall not be attributable to PMI and is solely the responsibility of the certifier or maker of the statement.

TABLE OF CONTENTS

LIST OF FIGURES AND TABLES

1

INTRODUCTION

In alignment with other PMI standards and practice guides, the *Practice Standard for Project Estimating* – Second Edition provides information on the activity of project estimating. This practice standard focuses on managing the estimating process and providing practical guidance geared toward project leaders, team members, and other stakeholders.

The audience for this practice standard includes, but is not limited to:

◆ Portfolio/program/project managers;

◆ Program and project team members;

◆ Functional managers/operational managers,

◆ Members of a program/project management office;

◆ Program and project sponsors and stakeholders;

◆ Educators and trainers of program and project management;

◆ Analysts;

◆ Scrum teams, scrum masters, and product owners;

◆ Senior management and/or any decision maker responsible for approving the estimate; and

◆ Individuals interested in program and project management and estimating in general.

This section provides an overview of this practice standard and includes the following subsections:

1.1 Purpose of this Practice Standard

1.2 Project Estimating Definitions

1.3 Scope of Project Estimating

1.1 PURPOSE OF THIS PRACTICE STANDARD

The purpose of this practice standard is to define the aspects of project estimating that are widely recognized and consistently applied based on generally recognized good practices.

◆ Generally recognized means the knowledge and practices described are applicable to most projects most of the time, and there is consensus about their value and usefulness.

◆ Good practice means there is general agreement that the application of the knowledge, skills, tools, and techniques to program and project management processes can enhance the chance of success over many programs and projects in delivering the expected business values, benefits, and results.

◆ This practice standard has a descriptive purpose rather than one used for training or educational purposes.

The *Practice Standard for Project Estimating* – Second Edition covers project estimating as applied to portfolios, programs, projects, and organizational estimating. Project management estimating affects portfolios, programs, projects, and organizational estimating—directly or by aggregation—and often has identical processes, tools, and techniques. While portfolios, programs, and organizational estimating—specific or within an organizational project management (OPM) context—will be covered at a high level, the principal focus of this practice standard will be on projects.

Sections 6, 7, and 9 of *A Guide to the Project Management Body of Knowledge* (*PMBOK® Guide*) [1][1] (Project Schedule Management, Project Cost Management, and Project Resource Management) are the basis for the *Practice Standard for Project Estimating* – Second Edition. This practice standard is consistent with those sections, emphasizing the concepts relating to program and project estimating. It is also aligned with other PMI practice standards as described in Section 1.5.

Figure 1-1 compares the purposes of this practice standard with those of the *PMBOK® Guide* and textbooks, handbooks, and courses. We recommend the *PMBOK® Guide* be used in conjunction with this practice standard because there are numerous cross-references to sections in the *PMBOK® Guide*.

---

[1] The numbers in brackets refer to the list of references at the end of this practice standard.

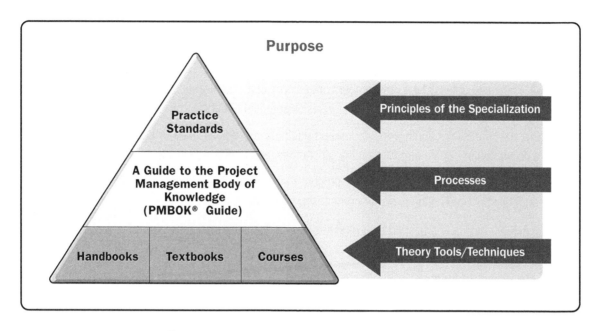

Figure 1-1. Hierarchy of PMI Project Estimating Resources

This practice standard emphasizes concepts fundamental to effective, comprehensive, and successful project estimating. These concepts are stated at a general level for several reasons.

Different programs, projects, organizations, industries, and situations require different approaches to project estimating. Project estimating is an appropriate process to apply to programs and projects of varying sizes. In practical applications, estimating is tailored for each specific program or project. There are many specific ways of practicing project estimating that follow the concepts presented in this practice standard.

These concepts are applicable to projects carried out in a global context, reflecting the many business, industry, and organizational arrangements between participants. These arrangements include joint ventures between commercial and national companies, governmental and nongovernmental organizations (NGOs), and the cross-cultural environments often found in these program and project teams.

Practitioners can establish procedures specific to their situation, program, project, or organization, then compare them with these concepts and validate them against good project estimating practices. In highly regulated industries or other environments, an independent project estimate may be mandated. Understanding the basis of those estimates, the methodologies, and the level of detail is important to project success.

1.2 PROJECT ESTIMATING DEFINITIONS

Important terms used in project estimating are defined as follows:

◆ **Estimate.** An assessment of the likely amount or outcome of a variable, such as project costs, resources, effort, durations, and the probability and impacts of risks or potential benefits.

◆ **Basis of Estimates.** Supporting documentation outlining the details used in establishing project estimates such as assumptions, constraints, level of detail, ranges, and confidence levels.

◆ **Baseline.** The approved version of a work product that can be changed only through formal change control procedures and is used as the basis for comparison to actual results.

These definitions are usually preceded by a modifier (i.e., preliminary, conceptual, feasibility, order-of-magnitude, or definitive).

Estimating, as described in the *PMBOK® Guide* and other related standards and practice guides, is comprised of three types of estimations, which will be elaborated on in this practice standard: quantitative, qualitative, and relative.

1.3 SCOPE OF PROJECT ESTIMATING

Project estimating is vital to successful portfolio, program, and project execution and the perception of success. Project estimating activities are a relatively small part of the overall program or project management plan and are first performed early in the program or project life cycle and repeated as the program or project progresses. The level of confidence is influenced by information available on, for example: market dynamics, stakeholders, regulations, organizational capabilities, risk exposure, and level of complexity. A program or project uses estimates along with the expected benefits to build the business case. Unrealistic estimates may compromise the ability of programs and projects to deliver expected value.

In addition to effort and resource estimation-based duration and cost estimations, project estimation is used in, but not limited to:

◆ Contingency reserve definition;

◆ Management reserve definition;

◆ Organizational budgeting and allocation;

◆ Vendor bid and analysis;

◆ Make or buy analysis;

- ◆ Risk probability, impact, urgency, and detectability analysis;
- ◆ Complexity scenario analysis;
- ◆ Organizational change management demands;
- ◆ Capacity and capability demand estimation;
- ◆ Benefit definition;
- ◆ Success criteria definitions; and
- ◆ Stakeholder management planning.

1.4 PROJECT ESTIMATING AND THE PROJECT MANAGEMENT PRACTICE

Even though estimates are initially developed at the onset of a program or project, it is important to think of estimating as a continuous activity throughout the program or project life cycle. The initial estimates are used to baseline the program and project efforts, resources, schedule, and/or cost. These estimates are then compared to the program and project benefit streams to determine feasibility. As the program or project progresses and more information is known, the estimates are continually refined and, subsequently, should become more accurate. This is consistent with the concept of progressive elaboration as described in the *PMBOK® Guide* and the *Agile Practice Guide* [2].

Additionally, the change control process is used to manage against the baseline cost and activity duration estimates. This continual process of reforecasting, based on new information and change controls, is why estimating is change driven and not a one-time event.

With the reported information during the project control phase, the project team will have enough data to refine the initial estimates and establish more accurate forecasts. This will create more effective action plans and allow a better understanding of program or project trends. There are many notable examples of final costs or schedules that were significantly different from the original estimate.

- ◆ In 1914, the Panama Canal ran US$23 million under budget compared with 1907 plans.
- ◆ In 1973, the Sydney Opera House was originally estimated at US$7 million. It was completed ten years late and the final cost came in at AU$102 million.
- ◆ In 1988, the Boston Big Dig was estimated to be US$2.2 billion. It was delivered five years late at a cost of US$14 billion, more than six times the estimate, due in part to flooding that destroyed all work and equipment, which was overlooked in the risk identification estimation steps.

◆ In early 1993, the London Stock Exchange abandoned the development of the Taurus program after more than 10 years of development effort. The Taurus program manager estimates that it cost the City of London over £800 million when the program was abandoned. The original budget was slightly above £6 million. Taurus was 11 years late and 13,200 percent over budget, without any viable solution in sight.

◆ In 1995, the Denver International Airport opened 16 months late and was an estimated US$2.7 billion over budget.

◆ The Federal Aviation Administration (FAA) launched the Advanced Automation System (AAS) program originally estimated to cost US$2.5 billion with a completion date of 1996. The program, however, experienced numerous delays and cost overruns, which were blamed on both the FAA and the primary contractor. According to the General Accounting Office (GAO), almost US$1.5 billion of the US$2.6 billion spent on the AAS program was completely wasted. One participant remarked: "It may have been the greatest failure in the history of organized work."

◆ In 1996, the Bellagio Hotel in Las Vegas, Nevada, was planned to be US$1.2 billion. The final cost was US$1.6 billion.

◆ In 2009, the London Crossrail project was estimated at £14.8 billion and scheduled to be completed in 2019. The project suffered severe cost overruns and is predicted to need an additional £2 billion in project finances.

◆ In 2011, the Mars Science Laboratory Rover was budgeted to cost US$1.6 billion. The final cost, when completed, was approximately US$2.5 billion.

◆ The new Berlin Brandenburg Airport (BER), started in 2006 and scheduled to be completed in 2010, was originally estimated at €2 billion. The updated estimate of the project is €7.3 billion and projected to be completed in 2020, ten years late.

1.5 RELATIONSHIPS AMONG THIS PRACTICE STANDARD AND OTHER PMI STANDARDS AND KNOWLEDGE AREAS

Estimating has connections to many other disciplines within program and project management, and it is an iterative process that occurs throughout the project life cycle. Figure 1-2 illustrates the relationships among this practice standard and other PMI standards and Knowledge Areas. Estimation is tightly integrated with the Project Scope Management, Project Schedule Management, Project Cost Management, and Project Resource Management Knowledge Areas.

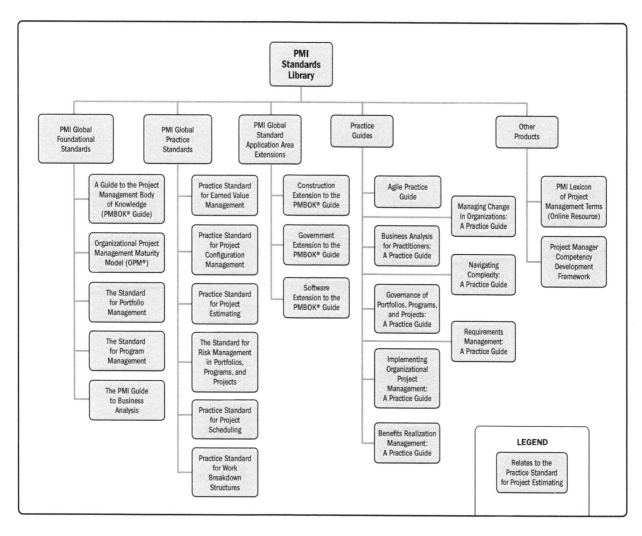

Figure 1-2. Relationship of Estimation Standard to PMI Standards Library

1.5.1 THE *PMBOK® GUIDE*

The sections in the *PMBOK® Guide* related to estimating are:

◆ **Section 3 on The Role of the Project Manager**

   ■ *Section 3.5.4 on Integration and Complexity.* Perceived complexity impacts the level of estimation confidence.

◆ **Section 4 on Project Integration Management.** Estimating is a critical aspect of creating the project management plan and performing integrated change control.

   ■ *Section 4.6 on Perform Integrated Change Control.* The process of reviewing all change requests; approving changes and managing changes to deliverables, project documents, and the project management plan; and communicating the decisions. This process reviews all requests for changes to project documents, deliverables, or the project management plan and determines the resolution of the change requests.

◆ **Section 5 on Project Scope Management.** The project scope is defined by the work packages that would be used for future estimates and the sizes of those activities, which are estimated for resources, durations, and cost.

   ■ *Section 5.4 on Create WBS.* The process of subdividing project deliverables and project work into smaller, more manageable components.

◆ **Section 6 on Project Schedule Management.** Develop Schedule is a process in the Project Schedule Management Knowledge Area that takes place in the Planning Process Group. Schedule management is a continuous and iterative process that requires reforecasting and refinement of the activity resource and activity duration estimates throughout the project. In an agile project, the story points are used to estimate the effort and the number of iterations.

   ■ *Section 6.2 on Define Activities.* The process of identifying and documenting the specific actions to be performed to produce the project deliverables.

   ■ *Section 6.4 on Estimate Activity Durations.* The process of estimating the number of work periods needed to complete individual activities with the estimated resources.

   ■ *Section 6.5 on Develop Schedule.* The process of analyzing activity sequences, durations, resource requirements, and schedule constraints to create a schedule model for project execution and monitoring and controlling.

◆ **Section 7 on Project Cost Management.** Determine Budget is a process in the Cost Management Knowledge Area that takes place in the Planning Process Group. Project Cost Management is a continuous activity that requires reforecasting and refinement of the cost estimates throughout the project.

- ■ *Section 7.2 on Estimate Costs.* The process of developing an approximation of the monetary resources needed to complete project work.

- ■ *Section 7.3 on Determine Budget.* The process of aggregating the estimated costs of individual activities or work packages to establish an authorized cost baseline.

◆ **Section 8 on Project Quality Management.** Quality is embedded across the estimating life cycle, including the incorporation of quality requirements, the continual monitoring of estimates, and taking lessons learned back into the estimating model. Includes the estimate of the cost of quality.

◆ **Section 9 on Project Resource Management.** Estimated activity durations may change as a result of the competency level of the project team members and availability of, or competition for, scarce project resources. Cost estimates should also include possible human resource rewards and recognition bonuses.

- ■ *Section 9.1 on Plan Resource Management.* The roles and responsibilities of who will make the estimates are defined.

- ■ *Section 9.2 on Estimate Activity Resources.* The process of estimating team resources and the types and quantities of materials, equipment, and supplies necessary to perform project work.

◆ **Section 10 on Project Communications Management.** Because there are many assumptions in creating an estimate, varying levels of information and confidence, as well as ever-changing forecasts, communications management is a critical component of managing estimates and expectations. Communications entails soliciting information as well as delivering it, and this is a key consideration for obtaining reliable data on which estimates can be based.

◆ **Section 11 on Project Risk Management.** Estimates are created based on an incomplete set of information, so there is always inherent risk involved that requires management. The impact and likelihood of each anticipated event are estimated in the risk register.

- ■ *Section 11.1 on Plan Risk Management.* The process of defining how to conduct risk management activities for a project.

- ■ *Section 11.2 on Identify Risks.* The process of identifying individual project risks as well as sources of overall project risk, and documenting their characteristics.

- ■ *Section 11.3 on Perform Qualitative Risk Analysis.* The process of prioritizing individual project risks for further analysis or action by assessing their probability of occurrence and impact as well as other characteristics.

- *Section 11.4 on Perform Quantitative Risk Analysis.* The process of numerically analyzing the combined effect of identified individual project risks and other sources of uncertainty on the overall project objectives.
- *Section 11.5 on Plan Risk Responses.* The process of developing options, selecting strategies, and agreeing on actions to address overall project risk exposure, as well as to treat individual project risks.

◆ **Section 12 on Project Procurement Management.** Procurement management includes acquisition of services or products that include resource, duration, cost, and quality implications.

- *Section 12.1 on Plan Procurement Management.* The process of documenting project procurement decisions, specifying the approach, and identifying potential sellers.

◆ Cost estimates and activity resource requirements are inputs to the procurement approach and are used to evaluate the reasonableness of bids. Often, the project estimate becomes the project budget after the contract negotiations.

◆ **Section 13 on Project Stakeholder Management.** Program and project success stakeholder expectations are mostly based on implicit or communicated estimations. Therefore, good estimations communicated in a timely manner are critical to perceived program and project success.

- *Section 13.3 on Manage Stakeholder Engagement.* The process of communicating and working with stakeholders to meet their needs and expectations, address issues, and foster appropriate stakeholder involvement.

1.5.2 *PRACTICE STANDARD FOR EARNED VALUE MANAGEMENT* [3]

Managing earned value starts with specifying the planned value for specific increments of work. Earned value is also a diligent way of monitoring and verifying the project actuals and forecasting and comparing them to the project estimates.

1.5.3 *PRACTICE STANDARD FOR WORK BREAKDOWN STRUCTURES* [4]

The work breakdown structure (WBS) defines work packages at a level of detail that enables an acceptable level of confidence for effort and resource estimation-based cost and duration estimations. The WBS also establishes essential relationships among key assumptions for scope, scale, and performance requirements at all levels used to support the various estimating methods. Finally, the WBS allows for estimation consolidation up to the program and/or project level.

1.5.4 *PRACTICE STANDARD FOR SCHEDULING* [5]

The schedule is created based on activity durations, derived from effort and resource estimations.

1.5.5 *THE STANDARD FOR RISK MANAGEMENT IN PORTFOLIOS, PROGRAMS, AND PROJECTS* [6]

Risk management uses qualitative and/or quantitative estimations and impacts all estimations as they are based on assumptions and uncertainty. Estimation is also used to define urgency and detectability of risks.

1.5.6 *THE STANDARD FOR PROGRAM MANAGEMENT* [7]

The sections in *The Standard for Program Management* related to estimating are:

◆ **Section 8.1 on Program Definition Phase Activities and Section 8.2 on Program Delivery Phase Activities.** These sections highlight the program management processes related to program and project estimating and assessment. Risk mitigation, for example, often results in additional work and cost, which need to be included as part of the estimate.

  ■ *Section 8.1.1.3 on Program Initial Cost Estimation.* A critical element of the program's business case is an estimate of its overall cost and an assessment of the level of confidence in this estimate.

  ■ *Section 8.1.1.7 on Program Resource Requirements Estimation.* The resources required to plan and deliver a program include people, office space, laboratories, data centers or other facilities, equipment of all types, software, vehicles, and office supplies. An estimate of the required resources—particularly staff and facilities, which may have long lead times or affect ongoing activities—is required to prepare the program business case and should be reflected in the program charter.

  ■ *Section 8.1.2.3 on Program Cost Estimation.* Program cost estimating is performed throughout the course of the program. A weight or probability may be applied based on the risk and complexity of the work to be performed in order to derive a confidence factor in the estimate.

  ■ *Section 8.2.3.2 on Component Cost Estimation.* Because programs have a significant element of uncertainty, not all program components may be known when the initial order-of-magnitude estimates are calculated during the program definition phase. It is a generally accepted good practice to calculate an estimate as close to the beginning of a work effort as possible.

◆ **Section 8.3 on Program Closure Phase Activities.** This section provides significant input for the Estimating Process Improvement stage as described in Section 6, Improve Estimating Process, of this practice standard.

1.5.7 *THE STANDARD FOR PORTFOLIO MANAGEMENT* [8]

Estimating impacts the portfolio life cycle as well as all portfolio management performance domains. Portfolio management practitioners, members of a portfolio management office, consultants, and other professionals engaged in portfolio management need to be aware of the relevance of selecting the proper estimating tools and techniques and the impact of estimating outputs within the portfolio performance domains, as described in the following sections in *The Standard for Portfolio Management*:

◆ **Section 3 on *Portfolio Strategic Management*.** Portfolio strategic management is the management of intended and emergent initiatives. It supports strategic thinking, is the basis for an effective organization or business unit, and assesses if the right thing is being done. The key terms in the context of estimating are:

  ■ *Portfolio funding.* Understanding the financial resources that stakeholders are willing to commit and the expected return on investment is critical in structuring the portfolio; and

  ■ *Portfolio resources.* Understanding the available resources committed to the portfolio assists the portfolio management team in structuring the portfolio while taking resource constraints and dependencies into consideration.

◆ **Section 5 on Portfolio Capacity and Capability Management.** The objective of portfolio capacity and capability management is to ensure that the portfolio's capacity and capability demands are in alignment with portfolio objectives, and that the organization's resource capacities and capabilities can support or meet those demands.

◆ **Section 7 on Portfolio Value Management.** Portfolio value management ensures that investment in a portfolio delivers the required return as defined in the organizational strategy. The investment and required return are estimations. Overestimating the investment may truncate further investments. Overestimating the return will create expectations that will destroy the perception of component success or even lead the organization to authorize components, which will not be able to produce the necessary return. The same concept is applicable to underestimating investment or return.

◆ **Section 8 on Portfolio Risk Management.** Managing risks below the portfolio level is usually viewed as exploiting opportunities and avoiding threats. However, when dealing with complexity at the portfolio level, the simple approach of avoiding threats and exploiting opportunities may not result in a complete balancing of portfolio risks. Risk and change should be embraced and navigated within an environment of complex interactions. Within this nonlinear environment, the portfolio management team addresses specific portfolio-level risks with the goal of optimizing value for the organization.

1.5.8 *THE STANDARD FOR ORGANIZATIONAL PROJECT MANAGEMENT (OPM)* [9]

Resource gap analyses, expert judgment, effort and resource estimation-based duration, cost estimations, and other estimations are used to develop OPM implementation or improvement plans. Capacity estimation helps to understand the viability of OPM initiatives.

1.5.9 *NAVIGATING COMPLEXITY: A PRACTICE GUIDE* [10]

Navigating Complexity: A Practice Guide and the impact of complexity on uncertainty and estimations are mentioned in all standards and the *Agile Practice Guide*. Complexity should be considered when estimating and communicating the level of confidence for estimations.

1.5.10 *AGILE PRACTICE GUIDE*

The *Agile Practice Guide* describes a context of program and project management with a recognized high impact on most program and project management aspects, including estimating. Agile practices and life cycles are termed *adaptive practices and life cycles* and generally embed risk mitigation practices that are merged with estimation and work practices. The merge of these practices leverages the speed of rough order of magnitude (ROM) estimates, such as relative estimation.

1.5.11 *THE PMI GUIDE TO BUSINESS ANALYSIS (INCLUDES: THE STANDARD FOR BUSINESS ANALYSIS)* [11]

The PMI Guide to Business Analysis (Includes: *The Standard for Business Analysis*) is a basis for business analysis as a complementary activity to project management and is heavily integrated into estimation practices. Section 5 of this guide, Stakeholder Engagement, contains relevant material in subsections that parallel estimation activities conducted by a business analyst. In addition, Section 7, Analysis, of *The PMI Guide to Business Analysis* (Includes: *The Standard for Business Analysis*) discusses using estimation techniques in product backlogs.

1.6 SUMMARY

This practice standard is intended for portfolio, program, and project management practitioners and other stakeholders. This practice standard covers the aspects of project estimating that are recognized as good practice in most portfolios, programs, and projects most of the time.

This practice standard focuses on resource and effort estimations, duration and cost estimations, capability and capacity estimations, risk urgency, impact, probability and detectability estimations, complexity assessments, and other estimation-related themes. Project estimating is important because of the many direct linkages to other aspects of portfolio, program, and project management.

The management concepts of project estimating described in this practice standard may be tailored based on the specifics of a program or project. Experience indicates that perceived program and project success directly correlates with the appropriate application of project estimating practices throughout program and project life cycles. This practice standard includes all project life cycles, including predictive and adaptive life cycles. *Adaptive life cycles* are agile, iterative, or incremental and are also referred to as agile or change-driven life cycles.

This practice standard uses the bicycle case study, included in other PMI standards and practice guides, to demonstrate the use and impact of project estimating.

2

CONCEPTS

Section 2 outlines the concepts of project estimating. This includes defining the scope, roles, and stages of project estimating. This section will also highlight important considerations, such as the causes of estimating variances, characteristics of an estimate, estimation methodologies, portfolio and program influences, governance, and industry practices around project estimating. Specific techniques are described in Section 4.

This section includes the following subsections:

2.1 Overview

2.2 Estimating Roles

2.3 Estimating Life Cycle Stages

2.4 Evolving Estimates

2.5 Use of Metrics and Available Data

2.6 Estimation Variances

2.7 Characteristics of an Estimate

2.8 Industry-Specific Practices

2.9 Case Study

2.10 Summary

2.1 OVERVIEW

This section introduces the concepts required to understand and estimate projects using the approach described in the *PMBOK® Guide*. These concepts are generally consistent with other commonly used approaches to project estimating across most projects and industries, although the terminology may differ. For the purpose of this standard, accuracy and precision are used interchangeably as a measure of closeness to the true value or model. However, there are specific domains where precision is distinguished from accuracy.

The concepts of project estimating described in this section cover:

◆ **Duration.** The total number of work periods required to complete an activity or work breakdown structure component, expressed in hours, days, or weeks.

◆ **Costs.** Estimating or assessing approximation of monetary requirements to complete the project.

◆ **Benefits.** Estimating or assessing the approximate benefits realizable by implementing the program or project.

◆ **Resources.** Estimating or assessing the estimate of resources required by the project and to complete project activities and work packages.

◆ **Nontask-related estimates.** Examples of nontask-related estimates include level of complexity, urgency, detectability, contingencies, and capacity.

◆ **Effort.** The number of labor units required to complete a schedule activity or work breakdown structure component, often expressed in hours, days, or weeks. Effort is based on scope and influenced by complexity, repetition, and risk as shown in Figure 2-1. Effort is typically measured in terms of labor units and should not be confused with duration. Duration describes the work periods necessary for a specific effort using the allocated resources.

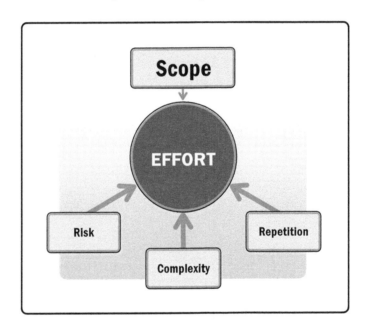

Figure 2-1. Effort

◆ **Level of precision.** This is the degree to which estimates will be rounded up or down (e.g., US$995.59 to US$1,000) based on the scope of the activities and magnitude of the project.

◆ **Level of accuracy**. The acceptable range (e.g., ±10%) used in determining realistic estimates.

The economic value of a worker's experience and skills is not always equal and varies from person to person. The human capital efforts required to complete project activities are expressed in the form of resource estimates, since units of measure can be used to estimate such efforts (e.g., labor units). Activity estimates may also include nonhuman efforts such as manufacturing line hours, equipment, and the materials required to complete the project activities. The basis of most cost and duration estimates is estimating the amount of effort required to perform an activity within the project scope, which may impact resource estimates. For example, if an activity requires eight labor units to complete, such an activity may be performed by one resource over eight calendar days or by two resources of similar performance over four calendar days. This relationship may not be linear. Cost is then calculated accordingly based on the assigned rates to the resources. Indirect costs can be included at the activity level or at higher levels. Figure 2-2 illustrates the possible sequence and interdependence among the estimate elements (effort, schedule, resource, and cost) and their respective key inputs. In an adaptive life cycle, effort may be an entry point.

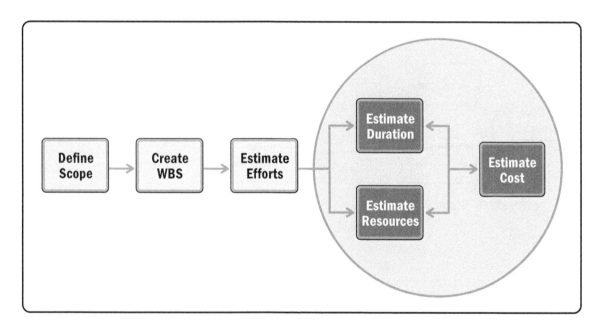

Figure 2-2. Estimating Elements

This practice standard uses the term *project estimating* to refer to all OPM components and is intended to review project estimating at a high level. Estimating benefits realization is an important dimension to consider in program and project management. Continuously estimating the value of the portfolio is a critical aspect of portfolio management. Effort, duration, cost, resource, benefits, and nontask-related estimates are applied to OPM components at the appropriate level of detail.

The three estimating technique categories are quantitative, relative, and qualitative (Figure 2-3). These techniques are categorized by the level of detail used in the creation of the estimate and discussed in Section 4.

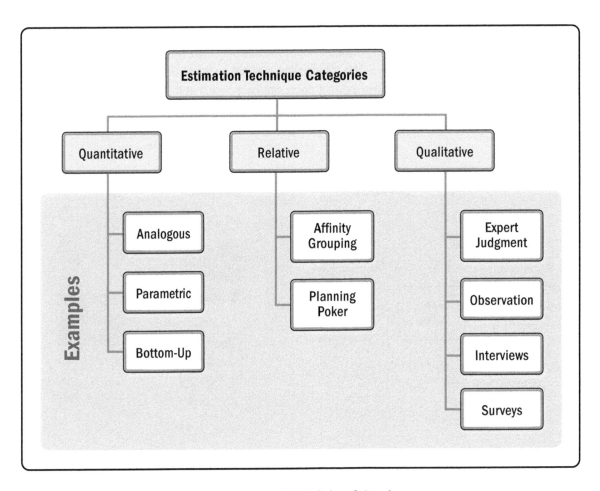

Figure 2-3. Estimating Technique Categories

2.2 ESTIMATING ROLES

The project manager is accountable for providing estimates that are as accurate as required and maintaining the integrity of those estimates throughout the lives of programs and projects. In order to improve accuracy, estimating should, whenever possible, be done by the person doing the work. There is the risk, however, that the person who will do the work will *sandbag* or pad the estimate for personal reasons. In change-driven project life cycles, it is incumbent on those doing the work to estimate the effort, or the anticipated value and benefits may be eroded.

Within the organization, several key roles are involved in project estimating (Table 2-1.). It is important that each individual fulfilling a project role is aware of his or her responsibilities in project estimating.

2.3 ESTIMATING LIFE CYCLE STAGES

There are three key stages in the project estimating life cycle:

◆ **Prepare to Estimate.** This stage of the life cycle is the creation of the estimating approach. This stage includes the identification of activities, determining the tools and techniques to be used for estimating, identifying the estimating team, preparing estimating inputs, and documenting any constraints and assumptions to the estimate (e.g., funding limits, resource constraints, or required dates).

◆ **Create Estimates.** In this stage, estimating effort, activity resources, activity durations, and costs are performed. The models and techniques for determining the estimates are explained in Section 4 of this practice standard.

◆ **Manage Estimates.** When the original estimate has been completed, validated, and baselined with the project team members and the project work has started, this stage of project estimating includes many activities that are used to manage the estimate, including change controls, calibrating the forecast, and comparing actuals to the baseline estimate. Governance of projects applies lessons learned to the estimating life cycle, such as calibrating the models based on actual values and maintaining checklists of components to include in future estimates.

Estimating processes are reviewed for improvement using information obtained during the estimation life cycle. Lessons learned and process control data are continuously or periodically analyzed and transformed in organizational process asset updates. Improvements are applied to all OPM components.

Figure 2-4 shows that the estimating stages are iterative and can be continuously improved. Estimates can be created at different phases of the project. A project estimate can be created in portfolio and program stages or at the *starting the project* phase as an early rough order of magnitude estimate to determine the viability of a project. An estimate can also be created in the *organizing and preparing* phase, with increasing levels of detail as the scope is elaborated.

Table 2-1. Key Roles in Project Estimating

Roles	Description	Responsibilities
Project sponsor	The project sponsor authorizes the budget as a project constraint and lays out an expected high-level schedule	• May provide rough order of magnitude budget and funding • May schedule estimates during project charter creation • Approve team estimates and modify budget and schedule accordingly • Approve/reject project changes throughout project execution • May change scope, backlog items, or priority of items in backlog
Project manager	The person accountable for the estimate, but not necessarily the one responsible for estimating	• Document estimating approach and plan • Coordinate/facilitate the team of estimators, assuring availability of relevant information in a timely manner, e.g., internal and external enterprise environmental factors (EEFs) • Review the estimates and initiate revisions if necessary • Aggregate the estimates from estimators • Identify and document risks and assumptions • Work with the appropriate financial resources to create cost estimates, contingencies, and alternatives (if appropriate). • Work with management to set expectations for stakeholders around estimates, assumptions, and risks • Notify portfolio, program and other project managers of potential impacts external to the projects • Is responsible for removing impediments to the team's estimating activities
Portfolio and/or program managers	Aggregation of estimates across the project within the portfolio (or program)	• Aggregate project estimates from project managers • Work with management to set expectations for stakeholders impacting benefits, estimates, assumptions, and risks
Estimators and subject matter experts (SMEs) (including project team members)	Individual or team responsible for estimating a specific activity in the project. Estimators should be team members from the project but may be people identified as experts in the area being estimated or other stakeholders	• Create estimates • Document assumptions and risks It should be noted that the estimator's experience will impact both the process of creating estimates and the output of that process.
Analysts	Individual or team who supports the project team	• Work as a team member or as external support, giving specific insights, e. g., business analyst and risk or cost estimator
Senior management	Individual or team who reviews and approves the project estimates	• Review and approve project estimate and impact on benefits
Customers of estimate	Individual or team who provides the scope to be estimated and accepts the estimates	• Provide the initial scope to be estimated • Work as a team member to develop the estimate • Review and accept the project estimate

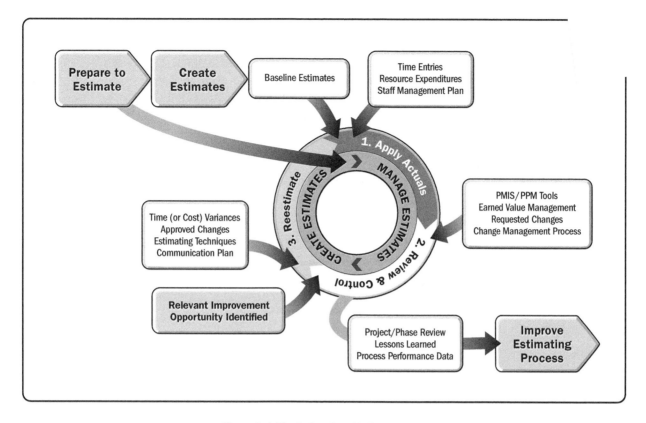

Figure 2-4. The Estimating Life Cycle Stages

2.4 EVOLVING ESTIMATES

All project estimates involve assumptions, constraints, uncertainty, and risk perceptions. Estimate confidence level is directly related to the activity definition and available information. Project estimates should be refined as information becomes available. Project estimating is iterative and evolving, aligned with the concepts of progressive elaboration. Figure 2-5 shows that, because of limited scope definition and available information, projects early in their life cycle have reduced estimate confidence and accuracy, thereby requiring a larger confidence range. As the project planning evolves, the scope is refined and a WBS and/or product backlog is created. As more information about the business case, requirements, desired deliverables, and acceptance criteria becomes available, the estimate can be fine-tuned to higher levels of precision and confidence.

For example, a project in the start-up phase may have a rough order of magnitude (ROM) estimate in the range of −25% to +75%. Later in the project, as more information is known, work product estimates could narrow to a range of −10%/+15%. In some organizations, there are guidelines for these refinements and the degree of accuracy that is expected. Contingency reserves are applied to estimates based upon available information and identified risks. As the cone of uncertainty (see Figure 2-5) shows, as the project gains more information, the need for contingency reserves associated with uncertainties in estimation should decrease. As with cost ranges, some organizations also have guidelines for contingency reserves to be used in the plan. Communication and stakeholder expectations management are important parts of managing evolving estimates. Project managers should help customers and stakeholders understand the concepts of evolving estimates and the associated risks, assumptions, constraints, and ranges.

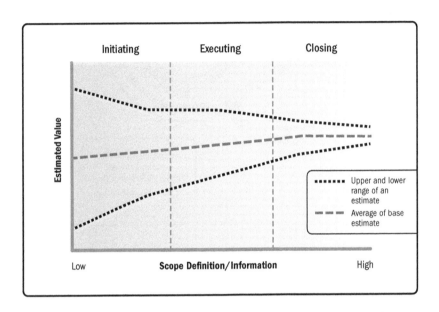

Figure 2-5. Cone of Uncertainty

2.5 USE OF METRICS AND AVAILABLE DATA

Available data influence the choice of the appropriate method. In preparing an estimate, for example, data points gathered from past projects, if available, may be used as inputs. With the analogous estimating method, estimates are derived from historical measures. With the parametric estimation method, estimates are derived by applying factor(s) to historical project measures. If no applicable data are available, a qualitative method is more appropriate.

Measures determined by an organization to be useful and reliable measures for evaluating project performance may be identified as metrics. Metrics are typically measures that are well-defined and captured on an ongoing basis to facilitate reliable comparison across projects. The availability of historical metrics and other lessons learned can be invaluable to efforts to improve the estimation process itself. The project manager captures such measures in order to evaluate project performance and refine estimates as needed throughout the life cycle.

2.6 ESTIMATION VARIANCES

The differences between the original and the adjusted estimates are called *variances* and tracking and recording them is recommended. As explained in the Evolving Estimates section, the more the team is involved in the work, the better they can understand the effort required to complete it—not only will the estimates evolve, they will also need to be adjusted. As a result of progressive elaboration, variances should become smaller throughout the project. If the variances are not reduced during the course of the project, the project team needs to take certain corrective actions.

2.6.1 PREDICTIVE LIFE CYCLES

The baseline used for tracking a project is approved early in the project life cycle, when the estimate is approved and documented in management plans. Variances between estimated and actual costs, resources, effort, and durations are normal in any project and occur for several reasons, for example:

◆ **Evolution of requirements.** Baseline project estimates are developed using a high-level view of scope and existing information, with many related assumptions made. As the project progresses in the life cycle (progressive elaboration), the scope is refined as the detailed requirements are defined and baselined. This elaboration may validate or invalidate prior assumptions. For example, in cases of under- or overestimated complexity or productivity, there is usually an impact on the schedule, resources, or cost.

◆ **The duration of the project.** The longer the estimates, the more inaccurate.

◆ **Approved change requests.** As the project progresses, changes to the original scope and schedule may be introduced by customers and other stakeholders and approved by the change control board (CCB). These requests may change the cost and schedule beyond the original baseline estimates so, although they are approved variances, they are still considered variances.

◆ **Operational problems or changing assumptions.** When creating the baseline estimate, assumptions are made about the activity resources, cost units, and durations. These assumptions can change as the project progresses or may have been incorrect. For example, a resource is assumed to be one rate, but the actual resource used on the project is more or less expensive. This will have an impact on the project cost. Another example could be a change in the source of materials.

◆ **Faulty estimating.** Due to the complexity and inherent uncertainty of projects, there are always occasions when a faulty estimate is produced. For example, neglecting to estimate a key component or area of work, mathematical errors, inaccurate data from an unreliable source, lack of team knowledge regarding the scope being estimated, lack of estimator experience, and not having enough time to estimate.

◆ **Padding.** A pad or a buffer is extra time or cost added to an estimate because the estimator does not have enough information or confidence. Padding undermines the professional responsibility of a project manager to provide a realistic schedule and budget. In cases when an estimator has uncertainties, these risks should be identified and reserves applied and/or the use of buffers considered.

Each of these causes of variance should be understood and managed throughout the project life cycle. The techniques include tracking the progress against the current baseline, rebaselining upon change management approvals, updating the assumption log, documenting lessons learned, and managing the risk register and risk management plan as new risks are identified.

2.6.2 ADAPTIVE LIFE CYCLES

The causes for variances are similar, although projects are planned and executed to more easily accept and adapt to scope or resource changes, for example:

◆ **Rough order of magnitude (ROM) variances.** During initial planning, the project team determines the number of iterations and their durations by approximating the effort needed. ROM estimates are replaced with other estimating methods not long after initial planning (e.g., relative estimating), which typically uses story points with Fibonacci, T-shirt sizes, and so forth.

◆ **One-point estimating variances**. The estimate may be based on expert judgment, historical information, or just a guess. One-point estimates allow for quick calculation but encourage people to pad estimates in response to risks and uncertainties.

◆ **Relative estimation**. In change-driven approaches, the upfront planning cycle is usually shorter and initial requirements are captured in much less detail. The estimate of effort to fulfill each requirement is often expressed in relative terms (e.g., story points) rather than in absolute terms (e.g., effort hours). Typically, the project team performs this estimating activity in a collaborative fashion. Because the cycles are shorter, the team can react to estimation variances faster.

◆ **Velocity**. The sum of relative estimates for the product features completed within a certain iteration allows the team to plan more accurately by looking at its historical performance. Velocity is specific to each team and cannot be used to compare their respective efficiencies. Velocity gets normalized over several iterations and is expected to remain unchanged subsequently. However, during the retrospective reviews in preparation for the next iteration, the team may adjust their velocity based on the resource availability or through improvements in the processes.

2.6.3 PORTFOLIO ESTIMATE VARIANCES

In the practice of portfolio management, estimates are focused on ensuring alignment of the portfolio and its components with the organizational strategy. Based on those factors, an organization leverages estimates to make an informed decision on project selection. ROM estimates are common, often determined by some combination of expert judgment and comparison to historical project efforts, if available. When a project is selected, the appropriate team will revise the initial estimates as detailed requirements are gathered.

2.7 CHARACTERISTICS OF AN ESTIMATE

Estimates should have several characteristics. Table 2-2 includes some of the basic elements that contribute to the creation of estimates for portfolios, programs, and projects.

Table 2-2. The Basic Characteristics of an Estimate

Characteristics	Descriptions
Requestor	The person or organization requesting the estimate
Target of the estimate	That which is being estimated (schedule, effort, resource, cost, risk, benefits, complexity, capacity...)
Level of confidence	The perceived level of confidence is the assurance in the estimate
Scope of the estimate	What was included/excluded from the scope of the estimate
Assumptions used	What information was assumed to be true for the purpose of deriving the estimate
Method utilized	How the estimate was derived, i.e., top-down, bottom-up, expert judgment, etc.
Estimator	Person or persons that contributed to the creation of the estimate or the subsequent review thereof
Version	As established in configuration management
Unit of measure	The unit of measure (time, money, risk)
Context of the estimate	Organizational capability and maturity, stability of the project context, such as market demands, political stability, exchange rates, industry, and other context-relevant characteristics

2.8 INDUSTRY-SPECIFIC PRACTICES

While the estimating life cycle stages are the same for all types of projects, there are some differences in the estimation metrics and models employed across industries. These variations are primarily related to the nature of the project's product, for example:

◆ **Software development.** The model used to estimate effort for software project tasks is influenced by the project life cycle employed by the team (e.g., predictive and adaptive) and the tools and techniques used to construct the final product. The extent to which project teams utilize expert judgment versus formal models also varies. Examples of model-based estimation methods include function point analysis (FPA), use case analysis (UCA), relative sizing, and story points.

◆ **Construction.** Different types of construction (industrial, commercial, residential, and healthcare) and the various trades (electrical, mechanical, and structural) have standard reference documents that provide general estimates for specific deliverables. The metrics used are primarily a combination of labor units and material costs. Parametric cost models for estimating within the construction industry use metrics such as square footage, location, and quality of materials.

◆ **Process-based industries.** Examples of process-based industries include manufacturing, mining, and petroleum refining. The metrics used in this type of estimation may include plant capacity, size of storage facilities, overall equipment effectiveness (OEE), labor units, and material costs.

◆ **Highly regulated industries** (e.g., pharmaceutical and nuclear). Bringing new drugs to the market is expensive, and the window for realizing profits from those investments is limited by patent exclusivity. Compliance with government regulations contributes significantly to costs throughout the development life cycle. Formal validation of manufacturing, clinical or laboratory facilities, and procedures are examples of factors that introduce additional costs. Few research projects will ultimately produce commercially viable outcomes, thus cost and schedule estimates that address inherent risks and anticipate compliance overhead are crucial to facilitating good investment decisions.

◆ **Government.** National, state, and local governments around the world regulate how individuals and entities conduct business in different ways. Projects in these spaces are subject to unique requirements, particularly about regulations, standards, contract bids, and procurement. The project team should have access to those familiar with the pertinent regulations and guidelines of the client government. A lack of competence in this area could result in missing contract opportunities, unanticipated costs for compliance with regulations, and schedule overruns, resulting in penalties.

◆ **Nongovernmental organizations (NGOs).** Within the context of NGOs and nonprofit-driven projects, estimations of value often focus on benefits, sustainability, and other nonquantitative dimensions.

2.9 CASE STUDY

Throughout this practice standard, specific practices will be demonstrated using a case study of building a bicycle. The case study is intentionally simple, demonstrating the use of multiple estimation techniques and the use of agile practices within the project. The entire case study is shown in Appendix X3, accompanied by examples of how each estimating stage is applied.

2.10 SUMMARY

Project estimating relates specifically to activity durations, activity resources, activity effort, activity cost, activity risk, and the project's benefits and value. The project life cycle determines the process and impacts the variances and roles of the project. Project estimates evolve and improve over the course of the project. The project estimate also evolves as the project moves down from portfolio to program, to actual delivery with further progressive elaboration. As a result of this evolution, a confidence range and contingency reserve can be applied. After a project estimate is baselined and the project progresses, there are several reasons why variances may arise. The project team should pay attention to the characteristics of an estimate and consider the differences in project estimating techniques across different industries and update the knowledge base by incorporating lessons learned.

3

PREPARE TO ESTIMATE

This section covers the Prepare to Estimate stage of the estimating life cycle and focuses on the creation of a project estimating approach. The objectives of this stage are to prepare to estimate and assure availability of all necessary resources to create the estimate.

The following subsections explain this stage in detail:

3.1 Overview

3.2 Prepare Project Estimating Approaches

3.3 Case Study

3.4 Summary

3.1 OVERVIEW

Before a project estimate can be created, documenting the project estimating approach is critical and usually performed during the initiation phase of the project. Documenting the approach helps the project manager and key stakeholders consider the many factors involved in the project estimating process and identify the resources required and techniques used to estimate the project.

Figure 3-1 shows the inputs and outputs for the Prepare to Estimate stage described in this section. Spending the appropriate time planning for an estimate will help to mitigate some of the causes of variance identified in Subsection 2.6 on Estimation Variances, specifically the evolution of requirements and faulty estimating.

3.2 PREPARE PROJECT ESTIMATING APPROACHES

The first step in the Prepare to Estimate stage is to obtain all relevant information to understand the context of what is being estimated as the information becomes available.

3.2.1 INPUTS

Inputs to prepare project estimating approaches are:

- ◆ **Project documents.** Project documents contain a wealth of information critical to the success of the project and improve estimate quality. Examples of project documents include:

  - ■ *Requirements documentation.* Describes how individual requirements meet the business needs of the project in the forms of user stories, use cases, bill of quantity (BoQ) if applicable and available, purpose of the project, technical characteristics, and solutions requirements.

  - ■ *Scope baseline.* The approved version of a project scope statement, work breakdown structure (WBS), and its associated WBS dictionary that can be changed using formal change control procedures and is used as the basis for comparison to actual results. In agile approaches, there may be no scope baseline. Using one agile approach—Scrum—the scope is defined by the set of user stories that have been chosen to be part of a release. These are initially sized at a very high level and refined as development and implementation of the requirement are undertaken.

  - ■ *Activity list, attributes, and schedule.* If the project has an existing activity list, backlog, and/or high-level schedule, these should be used in conjunction with the high-level scope as inputs to the Prepare to Estimate stage. Activity lists may also include activity attributes of associated data items that can be helpful in estimating, such as relationships, predecessors, and resource requirements.

  - ■ *Risk register.* A repository in which outputs of risk management processes are recorded. The team uses the risk register to help determine the areas that may require adjustments to project resources, time, or costs. For example, a technology that is new to an organization presents a risk, because team members may not know how to use it effectively and therefore it may require more time to plan, design, and test.

  - ■ *Resource calendar.* A calendar that identifies the working days and shifts upon which each specific resource is available. Any inventory of available resources is useful for estimating. Estimated activity duration is related to the availability, productivity, and allocation of resources.

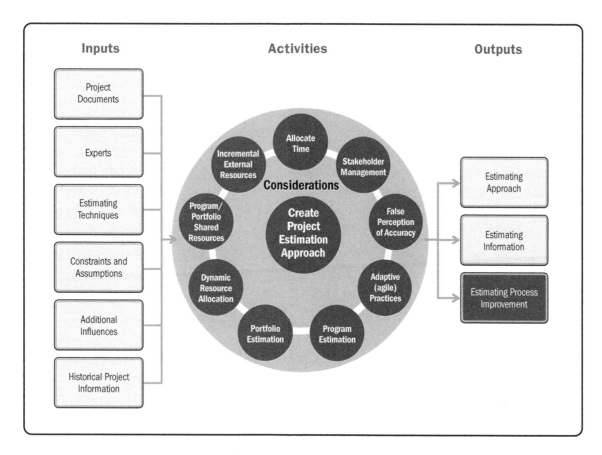

Figure 3-1. Prepare to Estimate

◆ **Experts.** Once the high-level scope of the project has been documented, the project team should identify the resources necessary to estimate the various parts of the project. Several techniques described in Section 4 of this practice standard utilize the knowledge and experience of key resources. Experts do not have to be dedicated members of the project team. The engagement of project resources increases buy-in of the estimates and generates a stronger commitment to meet the realization of those estimates.

◆ **Estimating techniques.** The project team should understand the available estimating techniques. These may be included in the organizational process assets that are gathered. By understanding the estimating techniques, a project manager will have the appropriate inputs available when it is time to prepare the estimate. For example, analogous and parametric estimates require historical information for projects, whereas a bottom-up estimate requires a detailed WBS and activity list. These techniques will be described in more detail in Create Estimates, Section 4 of this practice standard.

In adaptive or change-driven practices, such as agile, the estimation may be managed in iterations, and each iteration will produce a higher degree of confidence in estimation. Many of the techniques compare the relative effort of completing a new requirement to the relative effort of a previously estimated requirement or something known among team members. The objective is to produce a rough estimate appropriate for the immediate need, but in most cases not definitive.

◆ **Constraints and assumptions.** It is important to recognize the identified project constraints and assumptions. Some projects have fixed scopes, costs, values, and/or schedules, which may constrain the estimates. Identifying these constraints and assumptions allows the project manager to develop an understanding of the flexibility of various options when estimating (e.g., scope, duration, cost, or benefit) and which requirements cannot be changed. It is also important to note any early assumptions made about the project and document them in the project assumption log. Constraints may also arise from the organization, clients, technical/process requirements, or specific issues.

◆ **Additional influences.** The primary influences of a project, external to the specific project requirements, are organizational process assets and enterprise environmental factors. Both influences should be considered when estimating projects because they directly impact the activities, activity durations, and cost, described as follows:

- *Organizational process assets (OPAs).* Many organizations have standard processes, tools, and project management deliverables for managing projects. These assets should be understood so they can be planned for during the project estimating stage and included in the estimates. Examples include deliverables and processes included in the WBS that need to be estimated; estimating processes and standards required to be followed, which may include approaches for levels of confidence ranges and contingency reserve; and checklists of areas included in a project that need to be estimated. In the construction industry, there are databases for many items with unique codes that are continuously updated and maintained with vendors. These databases are key inputs for estimation.

- *Enterprise environmental factors (EEFs).* These include internal and external environmental factors that surround or influence project success. Examples include, but are not limited to, organizational culture, industry or government standards, and marketplace conditions. A more comprehensive list of enterprise environmental factors can be found in Enterprise Environmental Factors, Section 2.2 of the *PMBOK® Guide.*

◆ **Historical project information.** Once the high-level scope is known, the project team gathers available historical information on similar past or ongoing projects. This can be the basis for a comparison or starting point, which can be used in the analogous estimating technique. It may also be used to understand how to utilize lessons learned so that these are included in the project estimate. Examples of historical project information include effort, schedule, cost, resources, and other forms of documentation. IT and agile project managers should consider the age of historical information to determine if it is still valid to be considered as an input to their estimates. Using outdated data in developing estimates can be problematic in highly changing environments such as software development, where the data, tools, and techniques vary and evolve rapidly.

3.2.2 OUTPUTS

Once the inputs have been gathered, the project manager should document the project estimating approach about estimating activity effort, activity duration, activity resources, and cost.

◆ **Project estimating approach.** The estimating approach chosen by the team and the rationale for selecting the approach are important communication elements to help team members quickly understand a project and detect variances early. This information is often included in the project management plan and should be visible in all retrospectives on project progress. The documented approach for estimating effort, costs, activity durations, and activity resources includes a description of the project being estimated, the estimation techniques used, resource needs, assumptions, constraints, and timing of estimates, described as follows:

- *Scope of estimate.* What's included and excluded should be expressly identified and documented, along with a detailed list of assumptions. The scope of the estimate is not the same as the project scope and should not be confused with the project scope statement or scope baseline.

- *Organizational process assets (OPAs).* Companies that have standard organizational process assets may also have a list of mandatory deliverables for projects. These should be noted so that estimates are obtained for these deliverables within the project.

- *Estimating assumptions.* Explicitly state any assumptions about what is in the scope of the estimate and what is known and not known at the time of the estimate. These can include assumptions around the business case, the skills and availability of the team, and the project environment.

- *Constraints.* A factor that limits the options for managing a project, program, portfolio, or process. Constraints may be economic, legal, environmental, technical, or social and include specific data or costs for the project that cannot be altered. Specific constraints identified by the customer need to be identified and documented.

- *Estimation technique(s).* The project manager determines the best estimation technique(s) based on available information and identified risks. It is a good practice to use more than one technique to calibrate and compare those techniques. Section 4 in this practice standard outlines the scenarios in which each technique is best applied. This could include estimate rollup practices for related portfolios and programs.

- *Estimation confidence.* Identify what is needed to obtain a high level of confidence for the project estimate.

- *Contingency reserve planning.* State the approach for using a contingency reserve, including how it will be created, managed, and how it may change as the project progresses.

- *Risk assessment.* Assess the existing project risk register for risks that can impact the project estimate and how they are being managed.

- *Management and monitoring processes.* Document the plan for managing estimates, the timing and approach for reforecasting estimates, and the approach for monitoring the estimates and actuals. This should include the approach for metrics collection and reporting and the use of earned value analysis if being applied.

- *Improvement processes.* Document the approach for capturing and utilizing lessons learned, actual costs, and effort to improve the project estimating process.

Once the project estimating approach is selected, it is good practice to share it with team members and subject matter experts and obtain signoff from key project stakeholders. Even though these individuals may have helped select the approach, a review validates the communications and helps set expectations as to what is being estimated, what the evolving estimates mean, and how the estimating process will evolve. This practice also increases the sense of ownership, consciously or unconsciously motivating team members to work harder to meet the estimates.

◆ **Information and resources used to create the estimate.** While preparing the estimate, relevant information is gathered and will be used during the Create Estimates stage (see Section 4).

3.2.3 CONSIDERATIONS

Figure 3-2 depicts the challenges cost estimators typically face and the enablers available during the Prepare to Estimate stage.

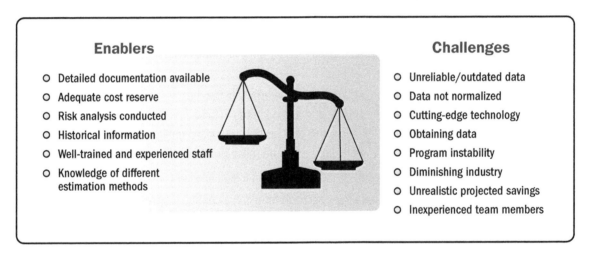

Enablers

O Detailed documentation available
O Adequate cost reserve
O Risk analysis conducted
O Historical information
O Well-trained and experienced staff
O Knowledge of different estimation methods

Challenges

O Unreliable/outdated data
O Data not normalized
O Cutting-edge technology
O Obtaining data
O Program instability
O Diminishing industry
O Unrealistic projected savings
O Inexperienced team members

Figure 3-2. Enablers and Challenges Cost Estimators Typically Face

The project team should consider the following while getting ready to estimate in the Prepare to Estimate stage (see Figure 3-2):

◆ **Allocate appropriate time to plan.** The project estimating process takes time to plan properly. Projects are often held to commitments from early project estimates, so it is important to spend an appropriate amount of time planning the estimate. This time should be considered an investment because it improves accuracy.

◆ **Proper stakeholder expectations management.** As described in Subsection 2.5, Use of Metrics and Available Data, the known information and subsequent confidence levels and ranges for estimates change over the course of the project. Therefore, it is important for the project manager to set expectations with stakeholders and sponsors early in the project and manage expectations properly over the course of the project as the estimate evolves.

Early on in a project, there are many unknowns; therefore, project estimates can offer a wide confidence range (see Figure 2-2) with many assumptions. Progressive elaboration makes estimates more accurate throughout the project life cycle. Recent historical information of similar projects is important because it contains valuable data about actual time, resources, and money spent on similar activities. It is important to explain this to stakeholders and provide them with an idea as to when information will become available and when higher confidence levels for estimates can be expected. Failing to manage expectations around early project estimates can result in stakeholders having a different understanding of the commitments for a project. This may cause resistance as a result of multiple interpretations of cost, resource, activity, or schedule estimates.

◆ **False perception of level of accuracy.** Early estimates usually involve many broad assumptions. However, sometimes project estimating techniques result in very specific numbers. This may give the impression of a higher accuracy or level of confidence during the project estimating stage than was performed. Project managers should consider rounding numbers to the next higher increments and providing ranges for early project estimates.

◆ **Adaptive life cycle (agile) project estimation.** Similar estimation and related management activities can be applied in the context of adaptive or agile projects. Such projects also depend on effort, cost, resource, and schedule estimates and reestimates throughout the project life cycle. Adaptive project life cycles apply the concepts more frequently due to the nature of repetitive shorter cycles and iterations. Recognizing and addressing project issues early and learning from previous iterations within the same project are key elements in estimate management.

◆ **Program estimate.** This section provides details on how to manage estimates of effort, cost, resources, and schedule in the context of program management. Similar activities can be applied to programs at higher and broader levels. The estimates of different project schedules within a program can be consolidated and used as input to estimate and update the program roadmap, especially when schedules of different program components change as a result of reestimates. Similarly, a change in a program component can result in a change of type or amount of resources allocated to it and other different components within the same program. Hence, cost may also require a reestimate. Moreover, program benefits are estimated and measured continuously.

◆ **Portfolio estimate.** Since the portfolio may be composed of different programs, projects, and operational activities, any change in the estimates of these components will have an impact on the portfolio they belong to in terms of roadmap, budget, or value. Portfolio value is estimated and continuously measured and monitored to ensure the organization is harvesting the highest possible value of its investment and adherence to the strategic plan. Portfolio-level estimates may also be validated using industry benchmarking for similar portfolio types or project categories.

◆ **Dynamic nature of resource allocation.** Resource availability is measured for a point in time and is subject to change for a variety of reasons: market forces, a change in an organization's priorities, or reductions in staffing levels. The strength of management's commitment to allocating a needed resource to a program or project shall also be assessed. Contingencies should be considered in case such resources become unavailable.

◆ **Internal versus external staffing.** Programs and projects may be staffed with resources internal to the organization, external (e.g., contractors/consultants), or some combination. External resources may bring skills or competencies the organization lacks or they may be used to fill in where internal resources are not available. Cost and schedule estimates should account for the process of onboarding external resources, including such activities as orientation, new user setup, corporate policy training, and procurement of computer equipment.

◆ **Portfolio/program shared resources.** Components within a portfolio and program may share similar resources. A change in any project within a program can result in a change of resources allocated to different components within the same program. One example of this scenario is: If a project is delayed and results in a delayed departure of some resources, it may cause another project within the program to delay its start if it depends on critical resources that are still held up by the delayed project. Consequently, the program manager may make changes to the program roadmap and change the assignment of resources to different projects. A second example within this scenario is: A project could be underspending, resulting in significant savings. This can lead to the inclusion of other, potentially lower-priority, projects in the portfolio.

The following activities based on and related to project estimating should also be considered:

◆ **Contingency reserve.** Time or money allocated in the schedule or cost baseline for known risks with active response strategies. Contingency reserve should be added to those estimates based on the risk analysis and available information at the time the estimate is created.

◆ **Organizational budgeting and allocation.** Planning for organizational budgets generally includes project funding as well as project revenues. These are typically based on project estimates, however organization-specific criteria for overheads are applied (e.g., corporate overhead, management, real estate, and taxes).

◆ **Vendor bid analysis.** Organizations often use internal or independent estimates when analyzing proposals.

3.3 CASE STUDY

Refer to Appendix X3 for relevant information regarding the estimating approach to produce a bicycle.

3.4 SUMMARY

The project estimating approach is identified and the goals for the project are outlined during the Prepare to Estimate stage of the estimating life cycle. This stage considers how the project will be estimated using techniques, organizational process assets, and experts and assembles those in advance of the estimation work. The Prepare to Estimate stage also documents any constraints and assumptions that need to be factored in and provides a level of confidence to management. Key project and historical information is gathered and used as input during the next stage, Create Estimates.

4

CREATE ESTIMATES

This section covers the Create Estimates stage of the project estimating process. The objective of Create Estimates is to apply estimating techniques to deliver project estimates with a known level of accuracy and considering inputs from other stages. If the project is a component of a portfolio or program, it may have an effect throughout the enterprise and this should be taken into account when creating and modifying estimates (Refer to Section 2, Figure 2-3, for more details on the three estimation technique categories). Appendix X3 contains a detailed example applying these techniques, including the case study.

The following subsections explain this stage in detail:

4.1 Overview

4.2 Use of Quantitative Estimating Techniques

4.3 Use of Relative Estimating Techniques

4.4 Use of Qualitative Estimating Techniques

4.5 Considerations

4.6 Case Study

4.7 Summary

4.1 OVERVIEW

With the project estimating approaches documented during the Prepare to Estimate stage, estimates can now be determined, as shown in Figure 4-1. Many different types of techniques are used to create estimates. Where practical and efficient, applying more than one technique is recommended.

Estimating techniques can be subdivided into three categories: quantitative, relative, and qualitative. Some projects may employ only one technique throughout the project, or various techniques may be applied at different stages in the project life cycle.

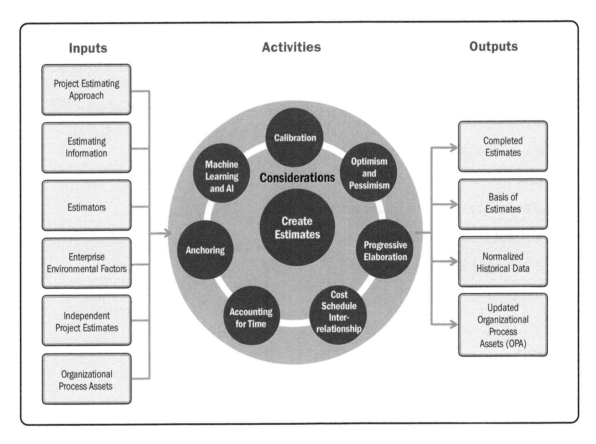

Figure 4-1. Create an Estimate

In adaptive project approaches, the daily reporting of progress mitigates the roughness of the estimate and any associated risk, because the estimate is refined daily or sometimes hourly. Within these practices the expectation is to deliver value rather than expend additional time trying to achieve a more accurate estimate. Each category of estimating technique yields its own success enablers and may have specific considerations that are identified within the technique. There are several general considerations that apply to all techniques and these are captured in Subsection 4.5 for readability and emphasis.

Figure 4-2 highlights the typical application of quantitative techniques in relation to the known project information, using the WBS as the reference base.

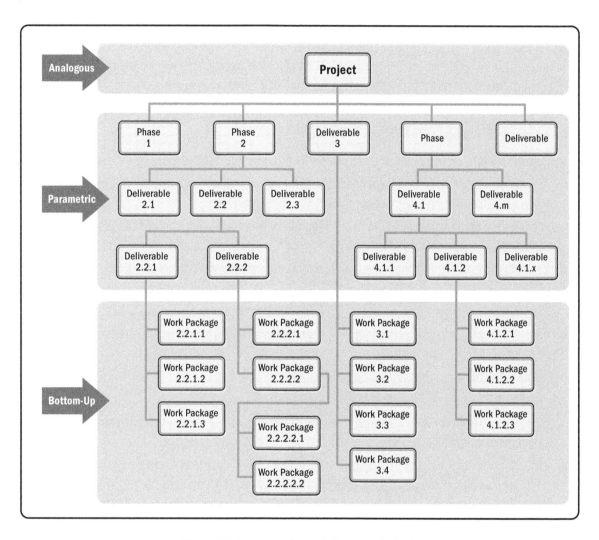

Figure 4-2. Decomposition or Rollup of an Estimate

4.2 USE OF QUANTITATIVE ESTIMATING TECHNIQUES

Quantitative estimating techniques are most widely applied to numerically estimate effort, duration, or cost. These techniques are not appropriate for all circumstances because applicable data, experience, or time may not be available. The main methods for quantitative estimating are analogous, parametric, and bottom-up and are described in more detail as follows.

4.2.1 ANALOGOUS ESTIMATING TECHNIQUES

Analogous techniques, also known as top-down estimating, are used when less information is available, the new project is very similar to a previous project, or the estimators are very experienced with what is going to be estimated. These techniques are preferred for early estimates when detailed information is not available. Analogous estimation is very common in portfolios in which a project placeholder may be needed to evaluate the entire portfolio.

◆ **Advantages of Analogous Estimating Techniques:**

- Require minimal project detail and are usually faster, easier, and less expensive to implement;

- Are useful when cost estimates are needed in the very early phases of a project. This is typically performed when very little information about the project, if any, is available;

- Focus on system-level activities such as integration, documentation, configuration management, and so forth. System-level activities are often ignored in other estimating methods;

- Typically receive greater commitment and support from senior management;

- Usually embody some effective features, such as cost-time trade-off capability, providing a global view of the project; and

- Allow the team to add new information as it becomes available to refine the earlier estimates and add detail as the project moves forward.

◆ **Disadvantages of Analogous Estimating Techniques:**

- Sometimes produce inaccurate estimates due to limited information (from a portfolio management point of view, which can result in undertaking poor investments or eliminating good investment projects during evaluation and ranking);

- Risk of using inappropriate historical examples (extrapolating data to fit another endeavor should be cross-checked for applicability, and many project failures can point to the root cause as being the data used. When there is any doubt, ensure the risks are identified and balance the use of this technique with one of the other practices to mitigate the risks);

- More contingency reserves are allocated for portfolios or programs;

- Often do not identify difficult low-level problems that are likely to escalate costs and sometimes tend to overlook low-level components;

- Provide no detailed basis for justifying decisions or estimates;

- Unable to baseline the project in order to monitor and control it due to lack of details specific to the current project, along with bias introduced by estimators, either optimistic or pessimistic.

◆ **Common Analogous Estimating Techniques:**

- *Ratio estimating.* This technique is interchangeably called equipment ratio or capacity factor. The premise of this technique is that there is a linear relationship between the cost of a project with one or more of the basic features of its deliverable. The basic deliverable features that will need to be quantified and used with this model are either physical attributes or performance characteristics. The ratios or factors may be derived from general industry data, personal experience, and/or enterprise-specific data. The following examples are illustrative but not necessarily universally applied concepts:

  1. An example of using general industry data for ratio estimating is a construction project, where the total cost of the project is estimated to be twice the cost of the material and embedded equipment.

  2. Another example of ratio estimating is when the cost for a high-level design of a system development project constitutes 30 percent of the total cost of the project. Secondly, the cost of human resources may constitute 50 percent of the cost of a construction project and 75 percent of the cost of a system and software development project.

  3. A third example (shown in Figure 4-3) applies a linear relationship among engineering hours, direct labor hours, and material costs.

  Ratio estimating presumes that there is a linear relationship between the capacity and cost, in that the ratio of two capacities is the same as the ratio of the cost of those capacities; for example, if the relevant capacity doubles, then so does the cost.

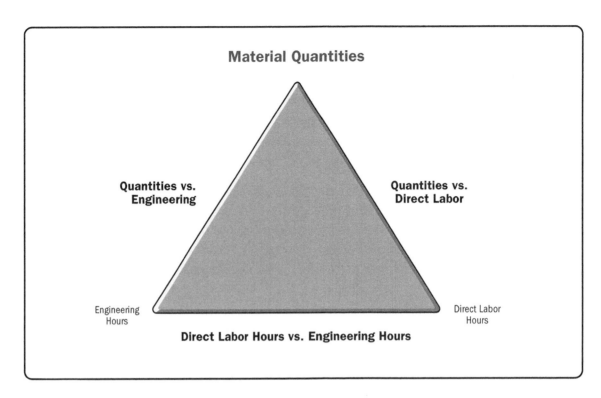

Figure 4-3. Estimate Triangle

- *Range estimating.* To increase the reliability and usability of the early estimates, the estimator should provide the most likely value along with the full range of all possible values for the final cost of the project. One subtle feature of this technique is that the accuracy of the estimate is embedded in the estimate.

  For example, a project team offers the following ranges for the costs of a new graphic interface software enhancement: three to eight resource months and US$150,000 to US$320,000.

- *Three-point estimating.* A technique used to estimate cost or duration by applying an average or weighted average of optimistic, pessimistic, and most likely estimates when there is uncertainty with the individual activity estimates. These methods are sometimes described as an independent subcategory of estimation techniques (e.g., *PMBOK® Guide, Sections 6.4.2.4 and 7.2.2.5*). However, the most common use is as a statistical method, applicable to any quantitative estimation technique to reflect the intrinsic uncertainty of the available data, most common in analogous estimations. An example of three-point estimating would be the triangular distributing represented by the formula of: $E=(O+ML+P)/3$ where

  E = estimate, O = optimistic, ML = most likely, and P = pessimistic, respectively.

- The *Program Evaluation and Review Technique (PERT)* is a more sophisticated form of the range-estimating technique. In this technique, three separate values for the cost (or duration) of the project or the cost of individual elements of the project are provided: optimistic, pessimistic, and most likely. With three values for the estimate of the cost of the project or of the individual elements, a certain degree of clarity is added to the estimate. This technique can also serve to normalize somewhat subjective data and potentially regulate overly optimistic estimator input. To temper the estimates, which may be overly optimistic, an adjustment routine using historical data can be used.

  PERT analysis uses a statistical probability outcome to calculate an expected proposed value based on a weighted average of the three values. It weights the most likely data by four times its value to reinforce its significance. The PERT formula is $E = (O + 4ML + P)/6$, which results in a beta distribution formula.

  The premise is that all estimates are forecasts with some uncertainty. A weighted average of the expected range of durations, work, or costs is a better predictor than a single most likely estimate. Project estimators tend to be overly optimistic. Using the PERT formula, the calculation may provide a result that is statistically more accurate. An example of this technique is when the project manager offers a most likely estimate of US$100,000 for developing a new medical testing device. To put the estimate in perspective, the project manager will highlight that, depending upon the materialization of identified project risks, the final cost could be anywhere between US$66,000 and US$210,000.

  Using the PERT formula, where O = $66,000, P = $210,000, and ML = $100,000, the project manager could propose a PERT value of US$113,000.

  The wider the range between the pessimistic and optimistic values, the greater the value is in using this technique.

◆ **Inputs to Analogous Estimating Techniques:**

Estimates are approximations by nature; therefore, estimate confidence levels are determined by the quality and availability of this input information:

- *Project estimating approach.* The project estimating approach decision or document identifies the initial decision making about the estimates and provides visibility into improvements and variances.

- *Estimating Information.* It is good practice to review the estimating information initially gathered to validate the quality of information and ensure it still meets the project estimating approach(es) selected for the project work. If the data are historical, they should be clearly adapted to the current project, culture, and situation to remove ambiguity and assumptions.

  In the development of an estimate, data should be expressed in like terms and agreed-on definitions of terms applied to the work at hand. Success criteria and the *definition of done* are critical to ensure the estimating information for different aspects in the problem domain can be compared with each other.

- *Estimators.* Estimates are highly individualized and best produced by engaging the people performing the work. Each individual works differently, best knows his or her capabilities in a given situation, and is most likely to produce the most accurate estimates. Estimators are also the most motivated to achieve what they have proposed. The risk in this case, as mentioned earlier, is that, if the estimator is going to be measured on achieving what he or she has proposed, he or she will pad the estimates to give him or herself a comfortable margin of error.

  In the absence of the actual human resource assigned to the activity, someone just as close to and familiar with the work being performed can provide the needed estimate. In this situation, the risk increases and the accuracy decreases. The estimate can be adjusted by the project team to allow for resource differences if no other option is available.

  A compelling argument for change-driven project life cycles (iterative, incremental, and adaptive) is the improved accuracy of the estimates by estimating *just in time* with the individuals doing the work immediately or in the very near future. Although an individual may be a very experienced resource, he or she may not be experienced estimating his or her work and may require mentoring or the use of relative estimating techniques.

- *Enterprise environmental factors and organizational process assets influences.* Enterprise environmental factors heavily influence the quality and accuracy of an estimate. Organizational process assets, such as estimating tools, techniques, procedures, or models should be identified when used. Estimating databases, productivity metrics, and/or published commercial information may be available, which could influence, accelerate, or assist in creating the estimates.

- *Independent project estimates.* Independent project estimates created by an independent (objective) party are required in some industries and highly regulated environments. However, there may be no requirement for the independent (objective) party to use the same methodology, level of experience, or work culture. This may result in a methodology that may differ significantly from the project team estimates. The project team should be cognizant of the basis of those estimates and strive to normalize the two so the use of an independent estimate is optimized.

◆ **Outputs of Analogous Estimating Techniques:**

- *Completed estimates.* Estimates for activity duration, activity resources, and costs are the key outputs of the Create Estimates stage. The proposed values are a prediction of the project outcome, not definitive values. Therefore, all estimates and their associated documents are dynamic and managed throughout the project life cycle.

- *Basis of estimates.* The amount and type of supporting details for the estimate vary by application area. Whatever the level of detail, the supporting documentation provides a clear and complete understanding of how the estimate was derived. This can include assumptions made, factors or units used, or comparative information. Identification of risks and items on the assumption log should also be included.

- *Normalized historical data.* A good estimation process should include time to review lessons learned and documented on other projects. Information in the lessons learned improves the estimate and other estimates during the project by increasing the accuracy with which problems are identified and quantification of the likelihood of occurrence and severity of their impact. Adjusting information from lessons learned is an important efficiency tool when projects are scalable. This information enables the success of current iterations and projects, especially when embedded in a portfolio or program.

  The adjustment needs to be performed in light of the differences between the proposed project and those projects that provided the basis for the model. The normalizing factors to be considered are: time of project completion, project execution location, changes in productivity metrics, quality metrics, and final specific product characteristics.

- **Analogous Estimating Considerations.** Projects held within portfolios or programs require alignment to those estimation expectations and value traceability. Project estimates roll up into the total portfolio or program estimate and therefore have a major impact on the overall estimate.

  In the development of an estimate, data should be expressed in like terms. This is typically accomplished by specifying data in terms of standardized units, such as a cost in a given currency in a given year, effort and efficiency with respect to a given benchmark, and so forth. Accounting for inflation is an important step in cost estimating. Cost overruns may result if a mistake is made or the inflation amount is not correct.

4.2.2 PARAMETRIC ESTIMATING TECHNIQUES

Parametric estimating techniques are designed to provide some mathematical equations to perform estimating. Parametric estimating is based upon historical information of very similar projects but takes into consideration scale differences by identifying unit/cost duration from past projects and scaling the information to the required number of units in the current project. These estimates are more accurate and reliable than analogous estimates but only if a statistical relationship exists between the variables used to calculate the estimate. The results of the estimates can be deterministic or probabilistic (Figure 4-4).

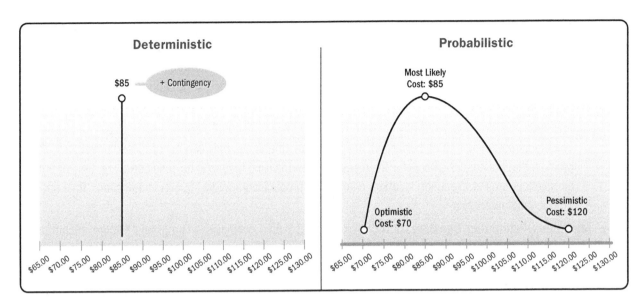

Figure 4-4. Deterministic versus Probabilistic Estimates

Project estimating relies on the most accurate information near real time. Techniques that produce more accurate estimates often require more detailed and voluminous information and take more time to develop, often decreasing the overall value of the project due to the increase in project costs. Rolling wave and change-driven project life cycles employ less detail up front to allow for making quick and rough estimates for the project during the very early stages. Refinement occurs closer to when the work is being done.

Activity durations or costs can be quantitatively determined by multiplying the quantity of work to be performed by the historical duration or cost of that work. For example, a laborer may take four hours to dig a three-foot-deep ditch that is 10-feet long. Using that same resource, it will take eight hours to dig a 20-foot-long ditch of the same depth. To apply that to cost estimates: If the labor rate for that resource is US$30 per hour, the labor cost for the 20-foot ditch is US$240.00.

The data that form the basis for calculations, the formulas used on those calculations, and the way the model gets updated are often proprietary to the organization. Factors, such as environmental or technical complexity or project risk, may also be applied to the overall estimate.

Using the parametric estimate, the estimator enters the relevant inputs, which vary from model to model. The model will then output values of cost, schedule, and resources for the project. The output also varies from model to model.

Parametric estimates take greater effort than gross-level estimating techniques and may be employed during rolling wave or just-in-time planning practices rather than up front in the beginning of a project.

- ◆ **Advantages of the Parametric Estimating Technique:**

  - More accurate and reliable than analogous estimates, yet simple to produce;
  - Receives greater commitment and support from senior management;
  - Creates estimates for many different projects; and
  - More estimators trust this method because it is tested internally and can calculate the capacity of labor or equipment according to the organizational environment.

- ◆ **Disadvantages of the Parametric Estimating Technique:**

  - Requires more time, effort, and cost to implement than analogous estimates;
  - Requires similarity among projects and tasks that are benchmarked to produce the parametric estimates;
  - Difficult to adjust for differences between projects (e.g., environmental, political, and cultural differences); and
  - Difficult to quantitatively estimate every cost or project event based on parametric benchmarks.

- ◆ **Inputs of Parametric Estimation.** The data and information needed for parametric estimation are significantly greater than those for analogous estimation. These mathematical equations are based on proven expertise, research, and industry-specific historical data (e.g., source lines of code [SLOC] in software development and cost per square meter in construction) blended with organization-specific standards and benchmarked against industry-specific standards.

- ◆ **Outputs of Parametric Estimation.** Parametric techniques use statistical relationships between historical data and other variables (e.g., square meters in construction) to calculate a detailed estimate for an activity duration, cost, and/or resource.

- ◆ **Parametric Estimation Considerations.** In environments where large amounts of accurate data are easily and efficiently obtained, parametric estimates can be the most efficient and accurate if the success enablers identified above are considered.

4.2.3 BOTTOM-UP ESTIMATING TECHNIQUES

Bottom-up techniques, also called deterministic or detailed estimating, are applied as the estimating tool of choice for estimating costs and resource requirements when detailed project data become available. Using this technique, the expenditure of every resource of every component of the project is estimated as a prelude to rolling up these estimates to the higher levels of the WBS and the total project. This technique will result in a transparent and structured estimate for the project that can be tracked and managed.

The bottom-up estimating technique is recognized to produce the most accurate and most reliable estimate, also known as the *definitive estimate*. Prerequisites to a bottom-up estimate are a detailed WBS, an activity list, and a comprehensive directory of project resources.

The project estimate is derived from the summation of detailed estimates for all the individual constituent components of the project. Using this technique, a detailed resource-by-resource estimate of the project can be performed. One of the many advantages of the resource-by-resource estimate is that it sets the foundation for informed change management when the project is constrained by a shortage of resources or, conversely, by a client request for a shorter project duration. Using the bottom-up estimating method, the cost of each component is estimated and the results are combined to arrive at an estimated cost of the overall project. This method aims at constructing the estimate of a *system* from the knowledge accumulated about the small components and their interactions.

The process begins by determining which resources are required to implement a specific lowest-level element of the WBS, known as a work package (see Figure 4-2). In some industries, some of the resources are not explicitly mentioned as part of the resource allocation or estimate. In this situation, it is recommended to list all the resources required regardless of the source of funds and mechanisms of payment. The list of resources can include all costs; labor; and other assets, including materials, embedded equipment, supplies, facilities, or implementation tools.

In summary, many different types of resources are required for a given project:

◆ Human resources or labor;

◆ Tools, facilities, and equipment for the workers;

◆ Embedded materials and equipment; and

◆ Licenses, fees, bonds, permits, and insurance.

The estimator uses the list of resources to assign the needed resources to each work package. For each resource, the estimator provides the optimum crew size for a function and the amount of time required by the optimum crew to craft the specific activities necessary to finalize the work package. For example, a work package could require three programmers (intensity) for five days (duration) and seven electrical engineers for one day. The cost of the work package is then calculated by summing the product of intensity, duration, and unit price of the resource.

Rolling up the resource estimates, duration of use, and cost of those resources to the intermediate levels of the WBS, and ultimately to the top of the WBS, will provide a resource-by-resource utilization estimate and the cost of those resources for the entire project.

◆ **Advantages of the Bottom-Up Estimating Technique:**

- Allows project team members to estimate the work for which they are directly responsible.

- Is more stable because the estimation errors in the various components have a chance to balance out.

- Can be the most accurate technique if the required estimating input information is available.

◆ **Disadvantages of the Bottom-Up Estimating Technique:**

- May overlook many of the system-level costs (integration, configuration management, quality assurance, etc.) since it focuses only on the WBS activity list.

- May be inaccurate if the necessary information is not available, especially in the early phase of the project or if there are hidden assumptions.

- Tends to be more time- and resource-consuming. May not be feasible when either time or personnel is limited.

◆ **Inputs of the Bottom-Up Estimating Technique.** The information used in other estimating techniques is required for bottom-up estimation. The completed quantitative analysis and any historical, retrospective, and definitive information are considered valuable inputs to the bottom-up estimating technique in particular. The detailed scope definition and schedule are also used as inputs.

◆ **Outputs of the Bottom-Up Estimating Technique.** Estimates for activity duration, activity resources, and costs are the key outputs of the Create Estimates stage. The proposed values are a prediction of the project outcome, not definitive values. This is an ongoing process that is managed and controlled throughout the project life cycle.

The amount and type of supporting details for the estimate vary by application area. Whatever the level of detail, the supporting documentation provides a clear and complete understanding of how the estimate was derived. This can include assumptions made, factors or units used, or comparative information.

◆ **Bottom-Up Estimating Considerations.** Bottom-up estimating takes time. In some environments, the speed of change may render this technique an unacceptable risk by leaving one open to competitive alternatives and delivering an obsolete product. In this case, top-down methods are used to provide high-level estimates. Rolling wave planning is then used to incorporate new information as it is learned, further refining estimates and iteratively elaborating with more detail as the project progresses. This acceptance of risk allows the project team to move forward and react quicker to market demands and adversity.

4.3 USE OF RELATIVE ESTIMATING TECHNIQUES

The acceleration of change in our world has led to the need to estimate an outcome where no experience, data, or time is available. Many projects and teams have been highly successful by applying relative estimating techniques. Relative estimating techniques take advantage of the human capacity to compare *things* to other *things* and avoids the difficulty in comparing something to an abstract concept (such as dollars or days).

Relative estimating techniques are high-level estimating techniques that use information that is currently available and known to the group doing the estimating. Each team member collaborates with the other team members to find a common item to visualize. If everyone understands the comparative sizes of the estimation units, the technique is very quick and efficient. Because these units are specific to the team doing the estimating, it is highly advised that the team use unusual units of measure to differentiate the estimates from other estimating techniques. For this reason, teams employing relative estimating techniques often use estimating proxies to represent relative sizes, such as T-shirt sizes, rocks, buckets, or virtually anything they can agree is a sizing relationship. Relative estimating techniques are designed to be fast (faster than traditional techniques) and deliberately trade off accuracy for speed. Time that is typically spent on estimating, is now spent on creative work, adding a direct value to the effort. The three estimating technique categories (see Figure 2-3) are quantitative, relative, and qualitative and are categorized by the level of detail used in the creation of the estimate.

The use of T-shirt sizes (Extra Small [XS], Small [S], Medium [M], Large [L], Extra Large [XL], Extra-Extra Large [XXL]) is another way to think of relative feature sizes. One popular artificial quantification of nonnumerical units is to use the Fibonacci Series—using the T-shirt example, size XS has value 1, S = 2, M = 3, L = 5, XL = 8, and XXL = 13. Other measurement proxies include NUTS (Nebulous Units of Time), and foot-pounds. Teams may create their own estimation units. Commonly used methods for relative estimating are affinity grouping and planning poker.

◆ **Advantages of the Relative Estimating Technique:**

  ▪ Simple, easy, and the least expensive technique to implement;

  ▪ Suitable when detailed information is not available; therefore, it can add more value to portfolio management compared to detailed project management;

  ▪ Allows the team to contribute more to the estimating exercise, since team members feel more comfortable providing comparisons of estimates rather than committed definitive figures; and

  ▪ Using a nonnumerical estimating unit prevents management from inadvertently considering the estimate as a firm commitment to deliver by a specific time.

◆ **Disadvantages of the Relative Estimating Technique:**

  ▪ May produce estimates that cannot be compared to other projects or work;

  ▪ Can be difficult to apply to estimating highly complex tasks within projects; and

  ▪ Team members may not learn the financial value of the work being done and its impact on profitability.

◆ **Common Relative Estimating Techniques.** Relative estimation is the technique of estimating one item compared to another or its *relativity* and, while highly subjective, has greater accuracy in a given situation for the team estimating the work. Following are some of the more common relative estimating techniques:

■ *Affinity grouping.* When the number of items the team needs to estimate is large, using affinity grouping is a technique where team members simply group items together that they perceive are like-sized. *Sized* could mean effort, time, value, or any other measure the team agrees to use. This method is simple, fast, and can be used with inexperienced and experienced team members. Step by step, a facilitator (or project manager) facilitates the team doing the work to find common ground (see Figure 4-5):

   ○ **Step 1.** The first item to be estimated is read to the team members and transferred to a visual place, typically a wall.

   ○ **Step 2.** The second item is read, and the team is asked if it is smaller or larger than the first item; placement on the wall corresponds to the team's response (larger is to the right, smaller is to the left).

   ○ **Step 3.** The third item is read, and the team is asked if it is smaller or larger than the first and/or second items; the item is placed on the wall accordingly.

   ○ **Step 4.** Control is then turned over to the team to finish the affinity grouping for the remaining items.

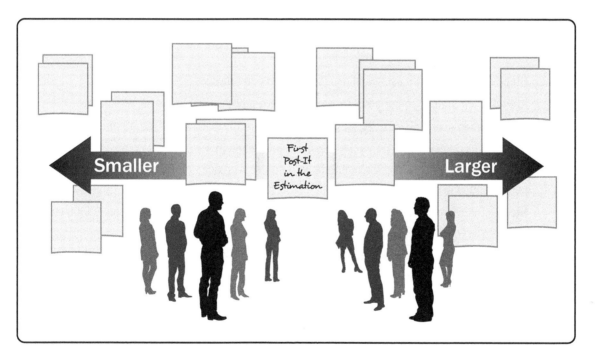

Figure 4-5. Affinity Grouping

Teams may choose to continue in the same fashion, placing one item at a time on the wall after group discussion. A faster way is to have each team member select an item and place it on the wall based on his or her own best understanding. This is done with all team members working in parallel until all items have been assessed and placed on the wall. Several hundreds of items can be estimated in a relatively short time. Once all items are on the wall, the team reviews the groupings. Items that a team member believes to be in the wrong group are discussed and moved if appropriate.

Once affinity grouping is complete, estimation unit values can be assigned. It is recommended that the team, when time permits, assesses the groupings and determines which identifying factors led one item to be more valuable than another. The categories/weighted values the team developed are important strategic enterprise environmental factors to be leveraged by portfolio management.

■ *Planning poker.* Planning poker is a common adaptive/agile estimating technique also used with other types of life cycles. Planning poker often uses a modified Fibonacci sequence series to assign a point value to a feature, epic, user story, or backlog item.

These numbers are represented in a set of playing cards (see Figure 4-6). Team members playing planning poker provide an estimate in the form of a point value for each item. The numbers on the cards represent values determined by the team to indicate the size of the effort. The steps in planning poker are:

○ **Step 1.** Every team has a set of cards and the sizing may be unique to that team while it exists.

○ **Step 2.** A perceived *owner* who is outside the *work team* (who does *not* get to estimate) presents the item to be estimated to the team.

○ **Step 3.** Team members ask questions of the *owner* and discuss the item.

○ **Step 4.** Each team member privately selects a card representing his or her estimate.

○ **Step 5.** When everyone is ready, all selected cards are revealed at the same time.

○ **Step 6.** If all team members selected the same card, then that value is the estimate. The cards typically vary, so the team discusses the estimate with emphasis placed on the outlying values. The intent is to understand why individuals selected a higher or lower value.

○ **Step 7.** The member who selected the lowest value explains why he or she selected the value.

○ **Step 8.** The member who selected the highest value explains why he or she selected the value.

○ **Step 9.** Each team member reselects a value representing his or her estimate based on the new knowledge. This is continued until the estimates converge.

○ **Step 10.** Should lengthy conversations result, team members may timebox discussions by using a timer, reselecting each time the timer runs out. This is continued until the estimates converge.

○ **Step 11.** These steps are repeated for each item to be estimated.

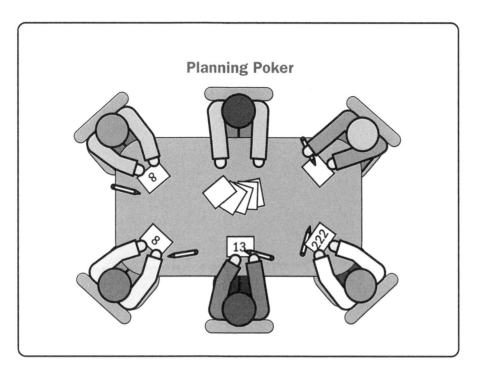

Figure 4-6. Planning Poker

Fibonacci numbers, like the nonnumerical values mentioned earlier, are used for several reasons. First is the notion that once teams eliminate time as the estimate base, they are less likely to demand more detail and pad estimates. Teams generally spend roughly two minutes on each item, allowing a backlog of 30 items to be estimated in one hour. Good practice is to limit the choices because this speeds up the process.

The sequence also provides the right level of detail for smaller and better-understood features, while avoiding a false sense of accuracy for higher estimates.

4.3.1 RELATIVE ESTIMATING TECHNIQUE INPUTS

Relative estimation techniques are popular because they require few inputs beyond a team focused on working together. Alternatively, the following should be considered for applicability and clarity to help the team normalize estimations quickly:

◆ Commonly used items in estimation current within the team culture; and

◆ Brainstorming methods and practices.

4.3.2 RELATIVE ESTIMATING TECHNIQUE OUTPUTS

The categories of outputs from relative estimating techniques are similar to outputs of other estimating methods. The lack of any standard outputs within the organization indicates that something may have been overlooked, for example:

◆ *Relatively sized elements visualized using an unusual character.* This makes it obvious that the estimate is not indicative of a quantitative or qualitative process. Naming mechanisms using objects is the most common method.

◆ *Sizing parameters.* The assumptions used by the team to develop their view of the sizing of the items are captured as risk elements and added to the assumption log for later understanding of the method employed.

◆ *Updated assumption log.* Assumptions used in relative estimating should be documented in the assumption log to ensure consistency across the project.

4.3.3 RELATIVE ESTIMATING TECHNIQUE CONSIDERATIONS

At some point, the team will have enough empirical data to develop their estimates. Educate the teams in the value of using these data to develop estimates. The quality and usability of the data will improve as more data points are gathered over time. As organizations grow and expand, the value of combining traditional and relative estimation methods will become evident and should be considered.

Leadership should embrace the concept of uncertainty in relative estimations in order to capitalize on the efficiency of rapidly creating a comparative list of work to be done and starting the work. This concept of delivering value is the core opportunity for relative estimation in that work is started as soon as the team feels they agree on the benchmark.

It is important to note that value measures do not have the same meaning across teams, even in the same organization. For example, a score of five from one team may not be equivalent to a score of five from another team.

4.4 USE OF QUALITATIVE ESTIMATING TECHNIQUES

Projects often have elements that are important but difficult to quantify. In cases where processes and/or perceptions are crucial or data not ideal, qualitative methods are appropriate and can be used in conjunction with quantitative methods. Qualitative estimates rely on understanding processes, behaviors, and conditions as perceived by individuals or groups. For example, how a project is perceived to have affected people's lives and how a training program is perceived to affect learning. Qualitative assessment can be rapid and often uses the same terms as relative estimates. Qualitative estimates generate textual (nonnumerical) estimates and range from unstructured to semi-structured techniques. Qualitative analysis uses subjective judgment based on unquantifiable information, as illustrated in Figure 4-7.

Figure 4-7. Quantitative versus Qualitative Methods

The purpose of a qualitative estimate differs from a quantitative one in that it explains and gains insight into and understanding of phenomena through intensive collection of narrative data.

The main methods for qualitative estimating are focus groups, expert judgment, interviews, and observations.

◆ **Advantages of the Qualitative Estimating Technique:**

- Does not require team members to be trained in estimating practices.
- Can predict changes in the future based on the experience and judgment of senior executives and outside experts.
- Provides management with the flexibility necessary to use nonnumerical data sources, such as the intuition and judgment of experienced managers, professionals, and industry experts.
- Is useful when there are ambiguous or inadequate data (for example, new software applications with no historical data of any kind).

◆ **Disadvantages of the Qualitative Estimating Technique:**

- Requires a large population to be statistically accurate.
- Can be subjective.

- Allows anchoring events where estimators allow the most recent events to influence perceptions about future events.
- Allows selective perception, as estimators ignore relevant information that may conflict with their view of how the future will unfold.

◆ **Common Qualitative Estimating Techniques.** Qualitative estimating techniques typically use qualitative data not easily reduced to numbers, are subjective, and depend on estimator experience. Use of these techniques is sometimes necessary by the nature of the estimated item and, when quantitative estimating would be a viable choice, often quicker and demands less effort. These techniques require understanding the context, people, and interactions, described as follows:

- *Expert judgment.* Expert judgment is defined as judgment provided based upon expertise in an application area, knowledge area, discipline, industry, and so forth as appropriate for the activity being performed. Any group or person with specialized education, knowledge, skills, experience, or training may provide such expertise.
- *Observations.* Estimations based on observations, with or without participation of the observer, use tacit knowledge of the observed group.
- *Interviews.* An interview is a formal or informal approach to elicit information from stakeholders by talking to them directly. The collected information can be used to formulate a common understanding of the estimates.
- *Surveys.* Surveys are written sets of questions designed to quickly capture accumulated information from a large number of respondents. The collected information can be used to formulate a common understanding of the estimates.

4.4.1 INPUTS TO QUALITATIVE ESTIMATING

Inputs for qualitative estimation are contact databases, survey results, interview notes, and documented observations.

4.4.2 OUTPUTS OF QUALITATIVE ESTIMATING

The outputs for this technique are:

◆ Estimates,

◆ Updated assumption log, and

◆ Updated baselines.

4.4.3 QUALITATIVE ESTIMATING CONSIDERATIONS

The questions being asked, in context with the given situation, make or break a qualitative estimate due to its dependence upon the interpretation of a single word. Conducting a survey or individual interview is an attractive option for lower-budget projects. The quality of the data, however, may not support the initiatives and is highly dependent upon the interpretation of the primary data gathered.

Surveys or interviews conducted over data sets much larger than the population impacted by the project outcome have significant value. Data reliability increases significantly with the amount of data when a small population is represented by a larger sample.

The initial data and the results of interpreting those data in estimation could be valuable in validating other estimating techniques.

Relative estimating is also inaccurately considered in many circles as qualitative estimating. Qualitative estimating techniques use narrative data, whereas relative estimating techniques compare values between an object of estimation and an agreed-upon baseline. Besides, quantitative estimates can be used as inputs to the relative estimating technique.

4.5 CONSIDERATIONS

4.5.1 CALIBRATION

Calibration is the process of determining the deviation from a standard to compute the correction factors. For cost estimating models, the standard is considered historical actual costs. The calibration procedure is theoretically very simple and involves running the model with normal inputs (known parameters, such as software lines of code) against items for which the actual cost is known. These estimates are then compared with the actual costs. The average deviation becomes a correction factor for the model. The calibration factor obtained is good only for the types of inputs used in the calibration runs. For a general total model calibration, a wide range of components with actual costs should be used. Ideally, numerous calibrations should be performed with different types of components to obtain a set of calibration factors for the various possible expected estimating situations.

4.5.2 OPTIMISM AND PESSIMISM IN ESTIMATES

Creating realistic estimates can be challenging. Optimism and pessimism are inherent in human nature and can lead to anchoring bias and poor estimates. There is often rework that can impact project commitments if not originally accounted for in the estimate. There are many reasons for optimism and pessimism, including:

◆ Level of experience may inadvertently cause exaggeration;

◆ Personal and business interests;

◆ Stakeholder expectations;

◆ Management pressure;

◆ Constraints (e.g., deadlines, financial limitations, resource availability);

◆ Ethical issues; and

◆ Organizational culture.

When project team members estimate durations for each work package, they often add some time as a buffer against the risk of unexpected issues. (Although the practice of deliberate overestimating—*sandbagging*—is unofficially decried and formally denied, it has the same effect as buffering and therefore is not addressed separately.) The result is a schedule with an oversized buffer due to a compounding effect, which, although normal, should be eliminated to develop a true picture of the schedule. Optimism and pessimism bias can thus have a profound effect on the accuracy of a given estimate, as shown in Figure 4-8.

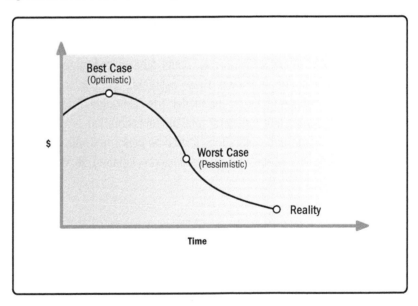

Figure 4-8. Buffering and Sandbagging Effect

4.5.3 PROGRESSIVE ELABORATION OF ESTIMATES

When estimating the level of effort required for any work package, activity, user story, or task, it is valuable to recognize that, as a discipline, estimating can be improved significantly over time. It is a common and often serious mistake for the project team to adjust estimates to justify customer, marketing, or management objectives rather than preparing estimates in an objective manner.

Estimates should be refined during the project to reflect additional details as they become available. The accuracy of a project estimate will increase as the project progresses throughout the project life cycle. Therefore, project estimating becomes an iterative process even if change-driven (adaptive/agile) planning practices are not intentionally applied.

In agile projects, velocity is a factor for progressively elaborating estimates. Velocity is a metric used for work done per iteration or over any other predefined period. It should be adapted to take into account the effects of the learning curve and is a frame of reference for the team. This metric is calculated by counting the number of units of work completed in a specified interval (timebox) determined prior to project start. Agile projects measure velocity frequently. Since points are only awarded for accepted products, the accepted work reflects a true measure of progress. Team members can revise their estimate of how long the project will take to complete if they know much about the work they are producing.

The estimates serve as the basis for portfolio, program, and project budgets. The plan and budget should be adjustable and fine-tuned, so the current versions of any of them are realistic and in sync with the revised estimates. Revisions of the plan and budget can happen any time during the estimating cycle and may occur after baselining. If this occurs, change control is utilized to manage the change.

4.5.4 COST–SCHEDULE INTERRELATIONSHIP

Development of the baseline estimate of resources and costs is predicated on certain assumptions about project pace. Project cost is often impacted by project duration. The project manager should always be sensitive to the fact that virtually any change in the project schedule and the amount of work completed in the project could trigger a change in project costs. For example, there could be an increase in project costs if a shortage of resources requires a longer duration or if the urgency of the deliverable necessitates a shorter duration. Earned value is one method used to monitor this relationship.

4.5.5 ACCOUNTING FOR TIME

If the project being estimated spans several years, the estimator or estimating models should consider factors such as inflation, which can include wages, resource costs, and materials. The project estimating team should consider inflators. Deflators should also be considered because falling prices could make a bid uncompetitive. The time-adjusted cost of a project is determined through a multiplication by the inflation or escalation rate. The time-adjusted cost is adjusted again by another multiplier to account for differences in project costs in the two locations. For example, labor rates, productivity, and work practices may vary by location. The time adjustment multiplier is mostly larger than one, although the location adjustment multiplier may be either larger or smaller than one. Time should also be taken into account with respect to the financial value of the project. Income that is realized later has a lower value to the organization than the same amount when it is immediately available. This feature can be accommodated by applying *net present value* to all financial inflow estimates. Take into account that sponsors could escalate and approve any deviation.

4.5.6 ANCHORING

Anchoring is a cognitive bias that impacts estimate quality. Anchoring (also known as *focalism*) describes the tendency for an individual to rely too heavily, and often unconsciously, on an initial piece of information offered (known as the *anchor*) when making decisions (Figure 4-9). During decision making, anchoring occurs when individuals use this initial piece of information to make subsequent judgments.

The focusing effect or focusing illusion is a cognitive bias that occurs when people place too much importance on one aspect of an event. This can cause an error in accurately predicting the utility of a future outcome and affects the way people intuitively assess probabilities. According to this heuristic, people start with an implicitly suggested reference point—the *anchor*—and make adjustments to reach their estimate. A person begins with a first approximation or anchor and then makes incremental adjustments based on additional information. These adjustments are usually insufficient, giving the initial anchor a great deal of influence over future assessments.

Those values near the anchor tend to be assimilated toward it and those farther away tend to be displaced in the other direction. Once the value of this anchor is set, all future negotiations, arguments, and estimates are discussed in relation to the anchor. This bias occurs when interpreting future information using this anchor. For this reason, documenting and revisiting assumptions and risks throughout the project relative to estimating are paramount. Education and awareness of anchoring are the best solutions to avoiding this bias.

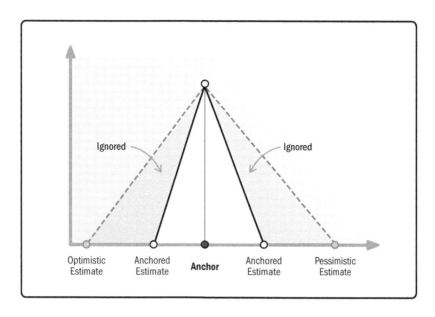

Figure 4-9. Anchoring

4.5.7 MACHINE LEARNING AND ARTIFICIAL INTELLIGENCE IN ESTIMATING

With increases in the use of artificial intelligence (AI) and machine learning (ML), estimation practitioners will be able to leverage advanced analytics techniques and tools and gain valuable insights into project estimating. Still an evolving area, over time the concepts of Big Data and Internet of Things (IoT) will enable project practitioners to perform estimating tasks more efficiently. Big Data will allow estimators to benefit from much greater data samples, whereas the IoT will allow projects to deploy measuring devices in areas and locations that are currently economical to measure. Using AI and/or ML shall not be misunderstood as implementing merely an informatics system; instead, both also rely on a proper knowledge management system.

4.5.8 COMMON SUCCESS FACTORS

Factors to consider, regardless of technique, are:

◆ Do not rely on a single cost, value, or schedule estimate.

◆ Use several estimating techniques or models, compare the results, and determine the reasons for any large variations.

- ◆ Document the assumptions made when making and updating estimates.

- ◆ Monitor the project to detect when assumptions that turn out to be wrong jeopardize estimate accuracy.

- ◆ Improve organizational processes: An effective process can be used to increase estimating accuracy and have an impact beyond the estimate and project.

- ◆ Maintain a historical database with metadata to explain the significance of the data.

- ◆ Maintain an assumption log.

- ◆ Identify and remove bias.

- ◆ A good plan

- ◆ Appropriate communication

- ◆ Clear requirements and specifications

- ◆ Clear objectives and goals

- ◆ Support from top management

- ◆ Effective project management skills/methodologies (project manager)

- ◆ Proper tool selection

- ◆ Suitable estimation technique

- ◆ Changes of company policy

- ◆ Testing

- ◆ Training

- ◆ Good quality management

4.6 CASE STUDY

Appendix X3 provides an example of an estimate used to produce a bicycle and update project documents.

4.7 SUMMARY

The project estimating process develops a prediction of how many resources the project will use, project cost, project value, and how long it will take to complete. The estimating techniques used may differ based on the amount of time allocated for the estimating process, the amount of information available at the time of estimation, the industry, the application area, the complexity, and identified risks. Whatever techniques are used to derive the estimates, it is important that estimating always be performed by the people who will be doing the work or those most familiar with the work to be accomplished.

The various methods of estimating—quantitative, relative, and qualitative—allow teams to select the techniques best suited to the available data and technology and the culture of the work environment. Each technique has its nuances that enable success. Estimates can vary significantly, depending on the phase of the project life cycle in which the estimate was made and the tools and techniques used in the process. Therefore, it is important to compare and validate the actual cost and time to the estimates even if only one or two techniques are used. This will provide the necessary feedback to improve estimating quality in the current portfolio, program, or project or for future work estimating.

5

MANAGE ESTIMATES

The objective of the Manage Estimates stage is to outline the fundamental inputs, activities, and outputs about managing estimates appropriately throughout the life cycles of portfolios, programs, and projects. This section also describes an approach to managing estimates from initial estimates to completed portfolios, programs, and projects based on the consumption of actual time and cost in relation to the completed work. The ability to reforecast remaining cost and time in relation to required efforts to complete remaining work is also described.

Managing the estimates of costs, effort, time, and resources is an intricate and interdependent exercise. As planned resources are consumed, the actual values are documented and compared with the planned values. Variances from the plan should be reviewed, and a decision made as to whether or not to formally revise the plan; if yes, then revised estimates are incorporated into a rebaselined plan.

This section includes the following subsections:

5.1 Overview

5.2 Manage Estimates: A Living Plan Cycle

5.3 Case Study

5.4 Summary

Although this section provides details on how to manage estimates in the context of project management, similar methods can be applied to portfolio and program management, because both domains contain similar estimate components but at higher and broader levels. Similar estimate and related management activities can be applied to the adaptive project life cycle. Adaptive life cycles may apply the concepts more frequently due to the nature of repetitive shorter cycles and iterations.

5.1 OVERVIEW

The program or project manager actually monitors and controls the schedule, costs, and resources for the program or project, as well as the estimates, so the Manage Estimates stage and the monitoring and controlling of the project are considered one and the same.

For the purposes of this practice standard, the Manage Estimates stage compares actual consumption with the latest approved baseline, assessing the impacts, validating and, if needed, adjusting the estimates if the variances are due to errors in the estimates rather than to project performance issues. Reestimating should never be carried out in such a way that it can disguise performance shortcomings.

Once the initial estimates are created as defined by the organizational process assets and the Create Estimates stage, management of these estimates is undertaken by the project manager, project team, and other key stakeholders. The same applies for portfolio and program management. Figure 5-1 illustrates the inputs and outputs of the Manage Estimates stage described in this section.

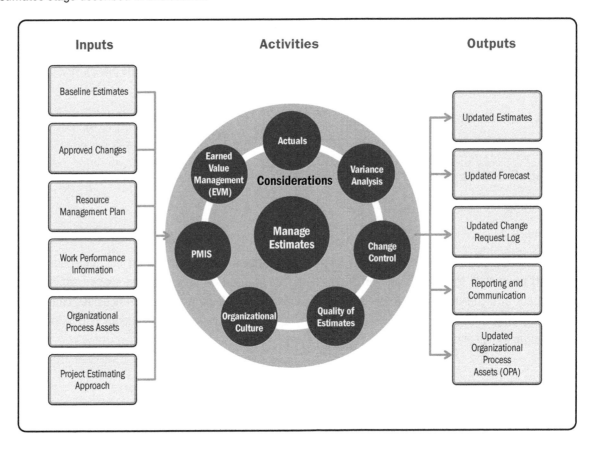

Figure 5-1. Manage Estimates

This approach is one of several industry good practices for managing project estimates. The concept includes the regular review of the estimate in a timely manner, adjusting for approved changes and reestimating or reforecasting.

5.2 MANAGE ESTIMATES: A LIVING PLAN CYCLE

This section covers the activities applied to the initial and revised estimates to properly manage and maintain the estimate throughout the project life cycle. The activities described in this section are good practices that can be applied to most projects, most of the time.

Figure 5-2 (steps 1 through 3) illustrates the process for the project estimate management cycle—from the time the initial project estimates are generated as project baselines, through a series of iterations where actual costs, time, resource consumption, and approved changes are applied. The results are reviewed and a reestimate for the portfolio, program, or project is created if necessary.

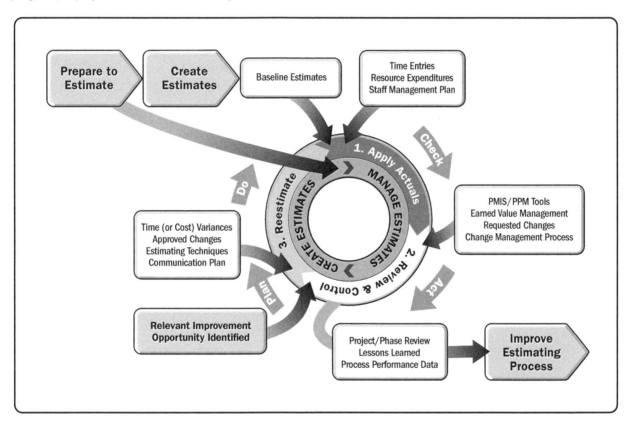

Figure 5-2. Estimate Management Cycle

◆ **Step one: Apply actuals.** Once the initial activity estimates are completed and baselined, the project manager or a selected project team member can begin to apply actual time, cost, and resource usage against the project management plan. The same also applies to portfolio and program management, because each of these management domains contains similar components at different levels.

   ■ *Effort estimate management.* It is crucial to measure if the original effort estimate to complete WBS packages defined in the project scope is correct or requires adjustment. A project manager may discover that an activity was underestimated in terms of efforts (e.g., ten work units instead of five), especially if similar activities will be performed throughout the project. Consequently, the project manager may decide to revisit the techniques used in the estimate or adjust the estimate to reflect the actual experience.

   ■ *Duration estimate management.* When there is a formal time entry process and the scheduling application is interfaced with the time tracking system, the actual time consumed should be updated automatically in the project management plan. If not interfaced, the time usage for each resource will need to be entered manually.

   In cases where vendors are employed, the actual time billed on the associated invoice should be reconciled. Estimations should apply information such as contextualized actual cost or actual duration.

   ■ *Cost estimate management.* As time is entered against the project, the resulting calculation of time consumed against the resource rate generates the consumption of actual costs.

   Special consideration should be made when adding nonlabor resource costs to the project. These costs may include such items as software, equipment, training, entertainment, team-building events, and fees or taxes, depending on the organization's cost accounting policies. If included in the original cost estimate, then consumption needs to be reflected appropriately throughout the project life cycle.

   ■ *Resource estimate management.* Throughout the project life cycle, resources are added or released, based on the resource management plan as outlined in the *PMBOK® Guide.* Consideration, in the form of an identified risk, should be given for normal and sudden staff turnover during the project. The resource roles, responsibilities, and competencies are defined, and the staffing management plans are detailed in the resource management plan.

   The resource management plan includes the procedures for staff acquisition and mobilization, resource calendars, staff release plans, and competencies and training needs. In the initial project resource estimate baseline, the known skill needs are documented, filled as close to the requirements as possible, and added or removed as needed. If the project runs according to plan, the resource estimate should reflect the proper use of resources throughout the project life cycle.

   This situation is not always the case. With the sudden turnover of a key resource, the project manager and project team may need to evaluate the availability of suitable candidates to fulfill the remaining workload. Should the resource be less competent, then the impact to the project schedule could be significant, because more time may be needed to complete the activities and deliver the scope. Conversely, if the replacement candidate possesses the skills of the previous team member, but the resource cost rate is significantly higher, this could impact the project cost estimate.

The availability, cost, and quantities of resources other than people (e.g., equipment, facilities, etc.) should also be tracked. The actual consumption is compared to that planned in order to determine if a reestimate is needed based on the degree of variance.

◆ **Step two: Review and control.** In parallel with progressive elaboration, project estimates should be scheduled for review on a regular basis to ensure proper controls are in place to identify variances. These variances can be caused by unmanaged project complexity, changes to requirements, or other project environmental variables that could impact the project estimate.

During the typical execution of a project, the project manager, project team, and stakeholders expect time and cost consumption to approximate what was stated in the project management plan derived from the baseline estimate. Each organization may have governance models or rules that describe this relationship. The actual time is applied with the rates factored in for each resource. Consumption of any resource costs other than human resources is factored into the project.

After applying actual time and costs or after assigning new team members, any time and cost variances should be compared to the project baseline for time and costs. If any variance is outside acceptable limits, then the project will need a more substantive reestimate, including any provision for scope, cost, resource, or schedule change control. The *Practice Standard for Earned Value Management* provides more details on the different types of variances and how they are measured.

For resources other than human resources—such as materials, equipment, facilities, travel, and expenses—tracking the use or consumption of these resources is equally important because they are included in the costs of the project.

Excluding approved changes, if at the weekly reviews the trend indicates significant over or under consumption, corrective action should be requested, documented, and communicated to the relevant stakeholders using the appropriate project control procedures.

The formal authorization of a change within any governance model includes: analysis and approval for changes in scope, cost estimates, schedule and duration timelines; resource staffing or skill competencies; and the decision as to whether or not the new estimate should be rebaselined.

◆ **Step three: Reestimate after applying actual time, cost, or change in resources.** When approved changes to scope, schedule, resources, or budget are introduced to the project and at certain key milestones—such as with a major deliverable at the end of a phase or an event—the project team conducts a formal review of the actuals used compared to the baseline. Any substantial cost variance or schedule variance is addressed through standard project management practices and is covered in the *PMBOK® Guide*.

The resulting variances also become inputs for reforecasting the project or the next project phase. The project manager and project team create forecasts on the remaining amounts of time, effort, cost, and resources needed to deliver the project or phase objectives. These forecasts are based on the current rates of consumption of time, effort, cost, and resources.

Schedule forecasts rely on actual time consumed to date, staffing management plans, and the remaining activity duration estimates.

5.2.1 INPUTS TO THE MANAGE ESTIMATES STAGE

Inputs to the Manage Estimates stage for activity effort, duration, resources, and costs will vary from portfolio to portfolio, program to program, project to project, and from organization to organization. Following are the six basic inputs required to effectively manage estimates:

◆ **Project estimating approach.** The project estimating approach, created during the Prepare to Estimate stage, defines the approach for managing and monitoring the project estimates and forecasts. This, along with the organizational process assets, should outline the plan for managing the estimate.

◆ **Baseline estimates.** The original baselines, plus or minus approved changes through agreed-on governance, are compared to the actual performance to determine whether they are within acceptable variance limits. The same also applies to portfolio and program management, because each of these management domains contains similar components at different levels.

For estimating purposes, the following are baselines for consideration:

- Cost performance
- Schedule estimate
- Resource histogram
- Activity effort
- Relative estimate baseline
- Estimation of benefits

These elements are interrelated. For example, a change in estimate of an activity effort will likely result in a change of schedule, cost, benefit, and/or resources estimates.

◆ **Approved changes to baseline.** Estimates are affected by approved requests for changes made to expand or reduce the project scope (i.e., effort); modify budget (i.e., cost); revise schedules (i.e., duration or time); or reflect a change in the makeup of the project resources (i.e., project team resources or other resources such as materials, equipment, facilities, travel, etc.). Since change control processes, inputs, tools and techniques; outputs for time, cost, scope, and efforts; and resources are covered in the *PMBOK® Guide*, this section will refer to those processes rather than reiterate them in this practice standard.

Typically, only change requests processed through the Perform Integrated Change Control process and approved should be considered when reestimating project efforts, resources, costs, or schedules.

Approved changes are included as outputs from the Perform Integrated Change Control process and are covered in the *PMBOK® Guide*.

◆ **Resource management plan.** As defined in the *PMBOK® Guide*, the resource management plan provides guidance on how project resources should be categorized, allocated, managed, and released. Following are some examples:

■ Through negotiation and team acquisition, appropriate human resources and associated competencies are assigned to the work activities.

■ When a critical resource skill is required and that skill is not part of the team or the person with that skill leaves the project, there is a risk of being unable to complete the task and a delay in completing tasks for that skill is likely to occur. This delay can impact the project schedule and the project costs until another individual with the required skill set is acquired.

■ If a resource is acquired with a competency less than planned for to undertake an activity, more time and/or more resources may be required to complete the tasks, resulting in reestimates of the project schedule and project costs. Resource competency requirements are defined in the roles and responsibilities section of the resource management plan.

The staffing section of a project's resource management plan also indicates which resource skills are needed and when to bring those resources in throughout the project life cycle. The timing for bringing on a resource and the utilization percentage assist in setting the resource profile to ensure an optimum amount of time is spent on the activities required to achieve project objectives.

Resources also include financial, facilities, equipment, and materials other than human resources. Quantities, costs, and scheduling for these resources should also be included in the initial project estimates based on planned activities. Consumption of these resources needs to be considered and tracked along with human resources:

◆ **Work performance information.** The actual amounts of time, resources, and costs associated with achieving the project objectives are considered work performance information, also known as the *contextualized actuals*.

Human resources are typically associated with costs in that there is an hourly rate. As time is consumed, this rate translates into cost consumption. This applies to both contracted and internal positions.

■ *Contracted positions.* In contracted positions, there are three common types of contracts: time and materials, fixed price, and cost reimbursable.

   ○ For hourly contracts, the hourly rate is negotiated within the contract and is typically based on the levels of experience and competence. The amount of time consumed is reflected in the hours billed to the project and represented in an actual invoice that can be applied against the project when posted to an accounts payable system. The tracking of actual time from invoices is important, as some nonbillable time may also be charged to the project. However, unless clearly specified in the contract, nonbillable time should not be tracked against the project cost estimate.

   ○ On fixed-cost contracts, the cost of the project is set at an agreed-upon price with milestone or phase-end billing points; the amount of effort used is immaterial to the cost estimate, to a point. When schedules slip, a vendor may decide to put additional or different resources on a project, but the final cost to the client remains the same. Approved changes may adjust the cost and therefore change the estimate, but the amount of total cost is consumed regardless of the amount of time consumed. Because of this, tracking actual time from invoices is important only in determining the work effort for better estimates on similar projects in the future.

■ *Internal positions.* For internal employees, the rate may be combined into a blended rate rather than displaying the actual compensation of any employee. For example, some organizations have developed a tariff rate, often referred to as a *burden* rate, for internal employees to use in project budgets for a better sense of the actual costs of portfolios, programs, and projects.

Some organizations do not track the cost of employees for a project, preferring to consider their compensation as a cost of doing business. Although this is not uncommon, it tends to not accurately reflect the total cost of investment and, therefore, the return on investment in achieving project objectives.

For both contracted and internal positions, a time entry system (i.e., timesheet or time reporting) may be employed to track the actual time spent on the project, or time can be tracked by a project coordinator on a project spreadsheet. From the time entry system, the project manager can apply consumption of time against the project schedule.

Some organizations do not require employees to enter time. However, in order to obtain a valid and accurate schedule, consumption of actual time spent on each activity by all project team members is highly recommended. This will provide a more realistic management of the estimate for similar projects in the future.

◆ **Organizational process assets.** An organization's corporate knowledge base or process asset library may contain the organizationally approved methodologies, processes, procedures, and templates used for managing the schedule, costs, and resource estimates. The Manage Estimates stage is dependent on the processes and practices defined within the process assets library. Well-defined processes and procedures for estimate management and reporting enable more consistency in managing estimates, and identifying, approving, and communicating estimate changes to the project team and key stakeholders.

The processes describe the approach for using the prescribed templates. The templates provide a level of consistency across projects and the organization. Samples of templates used could also be available as outputs from lessons learned activities from previous projects.

5.2.2 OUTPUTS OF THE MANAGE ESTIMATES STAGE

The outputs of the Manage Estimates stage for effort, time, resources, and cost vary from portfolio to portfolio, program to program, project to project, and from organization to organization. Common outputs from this stage are:

◆ **Updated estimates.** Updated estimates include all project estimates—project efforts, project time, project cost, and project resources; these are interrelated and all should be assessed as to the impact of any change. The same also applies to portfolio and program management because each of these management domains contains similar components at different levels.

◆ **Updated forecast**. Managing a project estimate by viewing the forecast is a powerful performance management technique. The updated forecast is defined as the recalculation of the cost and time to complete the remainder of the project or phase objectives based on the actual consumption of resources to date. This may be iterative and reflect small incremental cycles.

◆ **Updated change request log.** Any updates to the list of project change requests, for example, approved, opened, and closed changes, are change log updates. These changes should include the quantification of the impact of time, effort, cost, or resources.

◆ **Reporting and communication.** To assure stakeholder engagement and acceptance, reporting and communications should follow the guidelines and processes as defined in the communications management plan.

◆ **Updated assumptions log**. Management of the estimates may reveal incorrect hypotheses or give rise to new assumptions.

◆ **Updated organizational process assets.** Includes any templates or forms that were updated while managing the estimates.

5.2.3 CONSIDERATIONS

Key considerations and generally accepted good practices for the activities in this stage include but are not limited to the following:

◆ **Actuals.** Capturing actuals is the practice of using the data in such a way so as to recalibrate models, reestimate the project, and reforecast the balance of the project. It is important to ensure that time consumption is charged on the actual activities performed for those situations when employees enter time themselves. It also supports effective business management by providing reliable data for project cost-benefit evaluation. This practice allows the organization to refine and customize the estimating methods of the organization, thus contributing to improved initial estimates for future projects.

◆ **Variance analysis.** Variance analysis is the practice of analyzing, understanding, and communicating the impacts of time, scope, cost, and resources and the interdependencies each has with the others. When the reestimate results in a significant variance, the sponsors or steering committee may determine that the entire project should be rebaselined or, in exceptional circumstances, canceled. In these instances, follow the approved change management control process.

◆ **Change control.** Following the established guidelines and organizational methodologies for project management change control assists in maintaining close attention to the changes in cost, time, and quality when the scope of the project changes.

◆ **Quality of estimates.** Adhering to the living estimate processes produces a quality of estimates that enables the project manager and project team to address and forecast changes to the schedule, activities effort, costs, and resources.

◆ **Organizational culture.** Management of estimates is influenced by organizational culture. If the organization is strict regarding compliance to tracking consumption of actual time and/or cost against project estimates and in reestimating and reforecasting when change occurs, then the organizational culture for managing estimates will ensure reasonably accurate estimations.

- ◆ **Project management information systems (PMIS).** These tools are software applications that provide the project manager and project team with the means to record completed work, actual time, cost, and resource utilization throughout the project. These tools enable the project manager to maintain ongoing information for managing the estimates. From the simplest to the most complex, these tools are: spreadsheets, backlog management tools, advanced scheduling software, and project portfolio management (PPM) tools.

- ◆ **Earned value management (EVM).** Earned value management is a very important part of monitoring the project in that it integrates scope, time, and cost. It is an early predictor and gives the project manager and project team an opportunity to manage the estimates and proactively manage the project. Once forecasts have been developed, then other tools and techniques such as schedule compression, what-if scenario analysis, adjusting leads and lags, performance reviews, and resource alternatives can be used or applied as needed corrective actions.

For more information on the EVM process, refer to the *Practice Standard for Earned Value Management*.

5.3 CASE STUDY

Appendix X3 contains the case study on the bicycle example. In this study, bicycle production has started, the work performance data are captured and contextualized, and the obtained work performance information is updated.

5.4 SUMMARY

The Manage Estimates stage assures that actual estimates reflect ongoing portfolio, program, or project performance.

If estimates are accurate and there are no changes to scope and planned efforts, there will be no need for reestimates, and portfolios, programs, and projects will be delivered on time and within budget.

Controlling schedule, costs, and managing the project team are project management processes covered in the *PMBOK® Guide*, along with the Monitoring and Controlling Process Group. In this section of the *Practice Standard for Project Estimating* – Second Edition, definitions are provided along with a recommended process (living plan process) that defines why, when, and how to reestimate time, effort, cost, and resources during the project life cycle.

The living plan process described in this section is based on several real-life experiences and good practices. As this practice standard evolves, additional good practices and real-life experiences will emerge and become incorporated into the recommendation for added depth. However, the estimating cycle is a valid model for other existing approaches and may be the basis for variations on the theme.

6

IMPROVE ESTIMATING PROCESS

The purpose of the Improve Estimating process is to improve the organization's estimating capability for the OPM components. This section includes the following subsections:

6.1 Overview

6.2 Assess the Estimating Process

6.3 Implement Changes and Share Lessons Learned

6.4 Considerations

6.5 Case Study

6.6 Summary

6.1 OVERVIEW

A key objective of the Improve Estimating process is to update the organizational process assets, especially but not limited to, the estimating processes, templates, tools, and other assets. The process is based on actual data and lessons learned and completes the cycle by communicating process updates and assuring consistent process use.

This activity incorporates, but is not limited to, lessons learned and empirical data to calibrate the models, processes, and results in more accurate estimates. Improvements should be identified and applied at any point in the program or project life cycle.

Businesses apply process improvement techniques, such as process reengineering, to operations to improve efficiency and effectiveness. These same techniques apply to improving the efficiency and effectiveness of the estimating process regardless of the method or technique applied. One technique is demonstrated in Figure 6-1 and includes standardizing, measuring, controlling, and improving.

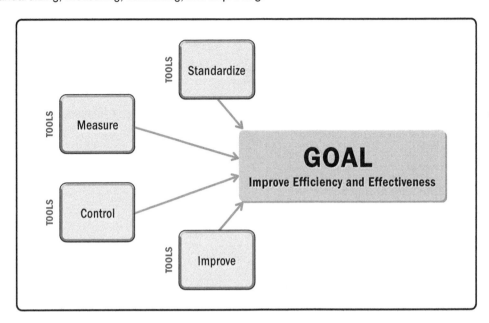

Figure 6-1. Process Improvement Steps

Continued realization of process application benefits is dependent upon the stewardship of the governance function in the organization. Choosing the best methodology for the improvement approach depends on the organization's structure, size, and complexity.

Studies show that most organizations that do not pursue continued improvement will regress and lose the value previously attained. For that reason, it is important to ensure that the estimation policy outlines a continuous improvement process. As indicated in Figure 6-2, there is a point where the actions that an organization takes will either progress with continuous improvement on the upward curve or regress to a less-than-desirable level of competency, as indicated in the downward curve.

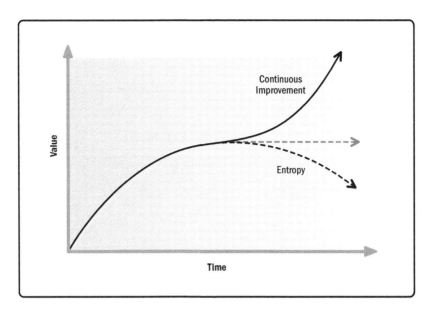

Figure 6-2. Need for Continuous Improvement

Managing and monitoring of the results of estimating process improvement actions are important to ensure that the levels of performance demanded have been achieved and to ensure that no unintended negative outcomes have resulted from the change. Figure 6-3 illustrates a long-term concept for overall process management methodology monitoring and management. Organizations plan and put in place the structure to perform this monitoring and improvement to ensure that the process management system continues to provide value and benefits to the organization. These benefits can be optimized on a long-term basis.

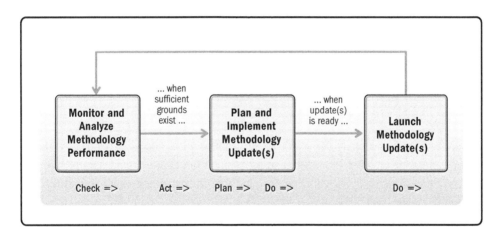

Figure 6-3. Process Management Methodology—Long-Term Model

6.2 ASSESS THE ESTIMATING PROCESS

To improve the estimating process, the team needs to gather the relevant information and plan for the improvement.

The example shown in Table 6-1 shows key questions that can be used to develop the estimating process improvement plan.

Table 6-1. Process Assessment Planning

Current State of Estimation Performance	Future State of Estimation Performance	Implementation Needs
KEY QUESTIONS	**KEY QUESTIONS**	**KEY QUESTIONS**
1. Has the organization's demand for estimation performance changed due to internal or external factors?	1. What processes should be developed to align with changes to the organization's demands?	1. Who do we need to engage?
2. What actions can we take to continuously align with the organization's demands?	2. Should an existing estimating method be leveraged or should a new one be developed?	2. What communication needs to be delivered to our stakeholders?
3. How quickly do organizational performance demands cascade to requirement updates in portfolios, programs, and projects?	3. How can governance and process improvement structures be streamlined so that decisions can be made more quickly?	3. What training demands arise from this asset improvement?
4. Is current estimation information available, timely, reliable, and actionable?	4. What membership, scope, and thresholds for the process measurement and control should be established?	4. How will we implement the improvements?
5. How many estimation practices are in use in the organization?	5. How can process performance information be improved to be available, timely, reliable, and actionable?	5. How do we validate training, communication, and implementation?
6. What actions can we take to improve performance?		6. How do we measure process application?
7. Are there risks that need to be considered?		7. Is there a need for corrective action to this or other projects?
8. How do we take advantage of opportunities?		8. How do we evaluate process improvement benefits?
9. How are decisions made on ongoing portfolios, programs, and/or projects?		9. How do we measure, control, and improve the improvement process?
		10. Is there information regarding performance, risk, or other areas that should be communicated?
		11. Do we have the appropriate level of stakeholder support and authority to implement?

The estimates are analyzed to identify opportunities for improvement once the necessary inputs are gathered. The assessment will determine whether the estimating process performs and meets the portfolio, program, project, or organizational unit-specific demands. It will also examine the process steps, context, and the assets, tools, and techniques utilized to formulate the estimate.

The findings of this analysis will be discussed in work sessions to determine their root causes. Root causes are identified by using techniques such as brainstorming, the 5 Whys, or the fishbone diagram. It is also valuable to staff these sessions with people who have problem-solving skills. An action plan for corrective or preventive actions needs to be developed to remedy the problems found in the current program or project.

The results of the analysis can also be used to update:

◆ Organizational process assets such as the organizational lessons learned to be shared with future programs and projects or future iterations of the ongoing project.

◆ Tools and techniques used in the estimating process, for example, historical information for analogous estimating, calibrated parametric models, and templates.

6.2.1 INPUTS TO THE IMPROVE ESTIMATING PROCESS

The following inputs assure success of the Improve Estimating process:

◆ **Program and project information.** The current program or project assets and results are assessed in search of improvement opportunities that can benefit current and future portfolios, programs, projects, or iterations. Project scope, risks, current estimates, and their assumptions are some of the objects of improvement opportunities.

◆ **Project estimating approach.** The current project estimating approach is the output of the Prepare to Estimate stage described in Section 3. Here it is used as an input.

◆ **Historical program and project information.** Historical program and project information is information collected from similar completed programs and projects and is described in Section 3.

◆ **Baseline estimates.** A baseline estimate is the first deliberate, detailed estimate of the effort, resources, cost, and schedule and is described in Section 4.

◆ **Updated estimates/forecasts.** Updated estimates/forecasts are estimates that have been made after the baseline and are described in Section 5.

◆ **Logs and registers.** Any project asset used to track and capture modifications, assumptions, and constraints within a portfolio, program, or project that suggests opportunities for process improvement.

◆ **Work performance data.** Planned versus actual estimate data include performance data for scope, schedule, resource measurement, and other elements expended on a program or project through a specific period.

◆ **Lessons learned.** Collecting and documenting lessons learned is a critical means of transferring knowledge to other programs, projects, or iterations. Lessons learned are generally collected at the end of a program, project, iteration, or after a critical activity or milestone. For adaptive life cycles, lessons learned are often captured during retrospectives often scheduled on a regular basis or conducted when a body of work is completed, such as the conclusion of an iteration or at the end of a project phase. To apply these lessons learned, it is essential that the information be easily accessible and institutionalized into the governing organization and its processes and procedures.

◆ **Organizational process assets.** Examples of organizational process assets are the established measure, model, definition, or criterion against which the estimating process is measured and are described in Section 5.

6.2.2 OUTPUTS OF THE IMPROVE ESTIMATING PROCESS

Many outputs from this process can be captured and applied not just to the current efforts but with future efforts in mind, for example:

◆ **Estimating process improvement action plan.** Having a great idea or a lesson learned from a retrospective is only as good as the actions generated. An action plan is a document—resumed or ample, simple or complex—depending on the organization's size and complexity, organizational change readiness, and estimation process change demands. The plan defines which identified improvement opportunities to implement and which to defer. This decision is based on change demands, cost, timing, change readiness, and resource availability. The plan should point to critical success factors; interdependencies such as logical, vertical, and horizontal; and prioritized improvement opportunities based on criteria such as interdependencies, value, assumptions, and constraints.

In addition to the technical changes, at a minimum, the action plan should include organizational change management aspects such as stakeholder engagement and mobilization, communication, coaching and training, and measurements of the proposed improvement results and impacts.

◆ **Organizational process assets update proposals.** Generally, the assets are not updated as part of the project work. Processes, policies, and procedures are typically established by the project management office (PMO) or another function outside of the project.

Where valuable, an organizational process assets update proposal should describe the identified estimation process inefficiency or failure, the identified causes, and the steps needed to improve the asset or its use.

6.3 IMPLEMENT CHANGES AND SHARE LESSONS LEARNED

Once the estimation process has been assessed and actions identified, the organization and project manager implement those changes and validate the associated metrics and measures.

6.3.1 INPUTS

Inputs to the Implement Changes and Share Lessons Learned process are:

◆ Estimating process improvement actions plan, and

◆ Organizational process assets update proposals.

6.3.2 OUTPUTS

Outputs to the Implement Changes and Share Lessons Learned process are:

◆ **Updated organizational process assets.** Updates to the organizational process assets can include, but are not limited to the following:

- Update to any artifact that defines the standard for estimating or affects the estimating process,

- Update to the estimating approach document, and

- Documentation of lessons learned for use in future projects.

◆ **Final report.** The final report can be resumed or ample, depending on the organization's size, complexity, culture, and improvement scope.

The final report documents the improvement by: consolidating assessment findings, updating proposals, results from test and update evaluations, implementation performance documented using key performance indicators (KPIs) or other means, and an integrated estimation review. This report can point to additional improvement opportunities.

6.4 CONSIDERATIONS

Considerations for the Implement Changes and Share Lessons Learned process are:

◆ **Senior management support**. Process updates need senior management support. The appropriate authority needs to be delegated to the practitioners who will be implementing the changes.

◆ **Investing the appropriate time and effort.** Investing the time and effort in search of improvements during the project life cycle is recommended. Preventive or corrective actions could positively impact current or future activities within the program, project, or future iterations, and the overall estimating process for the organization.

◆ **Consider the skill set.** It is important to note that the skill set needed to facilitate problem-solving sessions for determining the root causes may require resources not assigned to the current project. These resources should have facilitation and problem-solving skills. It is usually deemed wise to have an external resource conduct these sessions to eliminate bias.

◆ **Knowledge management.** Improvement findings, documented in the final report and/or other means, need to be shared using the organization's knowledge management approach to foster innovation, sharing lessons learned, integration, and continuous organizational improvement.

◆ **Stakeholder engagement.** Broad stakeholder engagement is critical for formulating the improvement initiative so all aspects are understood and addressed.

6.5 CASE STUDY

Refer to Appendix X3 for details about specific estimating process improvement opportunities that have been identified for the bicycle example.

6.6 SUMMARY

Improvement of the estimating process is iterative and encompasses the entire program or project estimating life cycle. It occurs during all program or project management processes in all Process Groups and receives inputs or produces outputs for most of the program or project management Knowledge Areas.

The organization should embrace continuous improvement practices, identify opportunities, and consolidate lessons learned. Where adaptive practices are employed, those lessons learned should be escalated to higher levels.

REFERENCES

[1]   Project Management Institute. 2017. *A Guide to the Project Management Body of Knowledge (PMBOK® Guide) –* Sixth Edition. Newtown Square, PA: Author.

[2]   Project Management Institute. 2017. *Agile Practice Guide.* Newtown Square, PA: Author.

[3]   Project Management Institute. 2011. *Practice Standard for Earned Value Management –* Second Edition. Newtown Square, PA: Author.

[4]   Project Management Institute. 2019. *Practice Standard for Work Breakdown Structures –* Third Edition. Newtown Square, PA: Author.

[5]   Project Management Institute. 2019. *Practice Standard for Scheduling –* Third Edition. Newtown Square, PA: Author.

[6]   Project Management Institute. 2019. *The Standard for Risk Management in Portfolios, Programs, and Projects.* Newtown Square, PA: Author.

[7]   Project Management Institute. 2017. *The Standard for Program Management –* Fourth Edition. Newtown Square, PA: Author.

[8]   Project Management Institute. 2017. *The Standard for Portfolio Management –* Fourth Edition. Newtown Square, PA: Author.

[9]   Project Management Institute. 2017. *The Standard for Organizational Project Management (OPM).* Newtown Square, PA: Author.

[10]   Project Management Institute. 2014. *Navigating Complexity: A Practice Guide.* Newtown Square, PA: Author.

[11]   Project Management Institute. 2017. *The PMI Guide to Business Analysis* (Includes: *The Standard for Business Analysis).* Newtown Square, PA: Author.

APPENDIX X1
THE *PRACTICE STANDARD FOR PROJECT ESTIMATING* – SECOND EDITION CHANGES

This appendix provides a high-level overview of the changes made to the *Practice Standard for Project Estimating –* Second Edition to assist the reader in understanding the changes from the previous edition to the current edition.

The *Practice Standard for Project Estimating –* Second Edition brings in current concepts used throughout the world in estimating portfolios, programs, projects, as well as operational activities. While many of the estimating techniques in use to today reflect what has been long proven in the workplace, some practices have fallen away and newer practices and techniques have added depth to project life cycle estimation. Adaptive life cycles, sometimes referred to as agile or Iterative, have become mainstream and hybrid life cycle applications more prevalent. This practice standard integrates new techniques, such as relative estimation, and eliminates less common practices, such as power estimating techniques.

In addition, this practice standard increased the use of examples and case studies to demonstrate and contrast the different techniques to increase experiential learning. In response to this need, this practice standard includes a fictional case study on a custom bicycle project to reflect the reality of mixed life cycles and project complexity occurring more often than not in our business world. In addition to the bicycle case study, examples of projects around the world encountering significant challenges in estimation are provided for discussion and to underscore the critical value that estimation practices bring to project environments.

Significant emphasis is placed on the use of *lightweight* adaptive estimation to educate both seasoned project managers in these new practices and less experienced project team members. The intent is not to provide an exhaustive list of practices and their variants. Rather, it is to illustrate the fundamental elements of the different types to allow the user of the practice standard to better select a practice that might more efficiently address the specific project environment and culture being faced. Another change is the increased emphasis on the need for individuals doing the work to estimate their own work and the recognition that estimation must be a continuous activity to fine tune and adapt to lessons learned and emergent situations.

Finally, the Glossary is updated to reflect the terms used in today's project world as well as a quick resource when using the practice standard.

APPENDIX X2
CONTRIBUTORS AND REVIEWERS OF
THE *PRACTICE STANDARD FOR PROJECT ESTIMATING –*
SECOND EDITION

This appendix lists, within groupings, those individuals who have contributed to the development and production of the *Practice Standard for Project Estimating* – Second Edition.

The Project Management Institute is grateful to all of these individuals for their support and acknowledges their outstanding contributions to the project management profession.

X2.1 THE *PRACTICE STANDARD FOR PROJECT ESTIMATING* – SECOND EDITION CORE COMMITTEE

The following individuals served as members, were contributors of text or concepts, and served as leaders with the Project Core Team:

Cindy Charlene Shelton, PMI-ACP, PMP, Chair
Richard Florio, PMP, Vice Chair
'Biyi Adeniran, PMP
Gerhard J. Tekes, PMO-CP, Scrum SFPC, PMP
Majdi Sabeg, PhD, PgMP, PfMP
Paula Ximena Varas, MBA, PMP
Ashley Wolski, MBA, Standards Product Specialist

X2.2 REVIEWERS

X2.2.1 SME REVIEW

The following individuals were invited subject matter experts who reviewed the draft and provided recommendations through the SME review.

Shyamprakash K. Agrawal, PMP, PgMP
Arnaldo M. Angelini, PE, CCE
Sergio Luis Conte, PhD, PMI-PBA, PMP
Theofanis Giotis, PhD, PMI-ACP, PMP
Mike Griffiths, APM, PMI-ACP, PMP
Adeel Khan Leghari, MBA, PMP, PgMP

Joshua Lerner, CSM, GWCPM, PMP
Timothy A. MacFadyen, MBA, MPM, PMP
Picciotto Merav, MA, PMP
Chris Richards, PMP
Dave Violette, MPM, PMP

X2.2.2 PUBLIC EXPOSURE DRAFT REVIEW

In addition to the members of the Core Committee, the following individuals provided recommendations for improving the public exposure draft of the *Practice Standard for Project Estimating* – Second Edition:

Ahmad Khairiri Abdul Ghani, MBA, CEng, PE
Juan Carlos Rincón Acuña, PhD, PMP
Jorge Omar Aguirre Tapia, PMP
Prescort Leslie Ahumuza, PMP
Jose Rafael Alcala Gomez, PSM, PMP
Emad AlGhamdi, MBA, PMP
Abubaker Sami Ali, MoP, PgMP, PfMP
Mohammed AlSaleh, PMP
Claudio Alves dos Santos, MBA, PMP
Nahlah Alyamani, PMI-ACP, PMP, PgMP
Angelo Amaral
Tony Appleby, MBA, CDir, PMP
Ayman Atallah, BE, PMP
Sivaram Athmakuri, PMI-ACP, PMI-PBA, PMP
Herman Ballard
Eduardo Bazo Safra, Mg, PMP
Nigel Blampied, PhD, PE, PMP
Greta Blash, PMI-ACP, PMI-PBA, PgMP

Farid Bouges, PMP, PfMP
Armando Camino, MBA, PMI-ACP, PMP
Panos Chatzipanos, PhD, Dr Eur. Ing
Nguyen Si Trieu Chau, PMP, PgMP, PfMP
Williams Chirinos, MSc, PEng, PMP
Timothy Cummuta
Mohamad Dawas, BSc, MSc, PMP
Danil Dintsis, PMP, PgMP
Christopher Edwards, MBA, PMP
Fereydoun Fardad, PMI-PBA, PMI-RMP, PMP
Elyes Farhat
John T. Farlik, DBA, PMI-ACP, PMP
Ahmed A Fikry, PMP
Gaitan Marius Titi, PMI-PBA, PMP
Hisham Sami Ghulam, MBA, PMP
Theofanis Giotis, PhD c., PMI-ACP, PMP
Scott M. Graffius, PMP
Simon Harris, CGEIT, AIPMO, PMP

Akram Hassan, PhD, MBA, PMP

Mohamed Hesham Youssef, PMP

Gheorghe Hriscu, CGEIT, PMP

Dmitrii Ilenkov, PhD, PMP

Antoine Karam, COBIT, PMI-RMP, PMP

Suhail Khaled, PMI-ACP, PMP

Taeyoung Kim, PMP

Rouzbeh Kotobzadeh

Prathyusha Ramayanam Venkata Naga Lakshmi, MBA, Btech

G Lakshmi Sekhar, PMI-PBA, PMI-SP, PMP

Arun Lal, BE, PMP

Lydia G. Liberio, JD, MBA, PMP

Medhat Mahmoud

Christian Moerz, PMP

Venkatramvasi Mohanvasi, BE, PMP

Felipe Fernandes Moreira, PMP

Syed Ahsan Mustaqeem, PE, PMP

Adriano Jose da Silva Neves

Habeeb Omar, PgMP, PfMP

Arivazhagan Ondiappan, BE, PMI-RMP, PMP

Paul Paquette, MBA, PMI-RMP, PMP

Heny Patel

Crispin ("Kik") Piney, PMP, PgMP, PfMP

P. Ravikumar, PMI-ACP, PMP, PgMP

Omar Redwan

Curtis Richardson

Bernard Roduit

Dan Stelian Roman, LSSBB, PMI-ACP, PMP

Omar A. Samaniego, PMI-RMP, PMP

Saravanaperumal K, ITIL, PMP

Walla Siddig Elhadey Mohamed, PMOCP, PMI-RMP, PMP

Mauro Sotille, PMI-RMP, PMP

Gerald Spencer

Prasanna Surakanti, MS EE, MSc

Tamiki Takayashiki, PMP

Laurent Thomas, DrSc, SPC4, PMP

Mohammed Thoufeeq

Micol Trezza, MBA, PMP

Daniel Ubilla Baier, MBA, PMOCP, PMP

Thierry Verlynde, MS, Coach, PMP

Michal Wieteska, ASEP, PMP

J. Craig Williams, PMP

X2.2.3 PMI STANDARDS PROGRAM MEMBER ADVISORY GROUP (SMAG)

The PMI Standards Program Member Advisory Group (SMAG) works under the leadership of the standards manager. We extend our sincerest thanks to them for their compelling and helpful guidance throughout the development process.

During the course of the committee's work, the following distinguished members of the PMI community served on the SMAG:

Maria Cristina Barbero, CSM, PMI-ACP, PMP

Michael J. Frenette, I.S.P., SMC, MCITP, PMP

Brian Grafsgaard, CSM, PMP, PgMP, PfMP

David Gunner, MSc, PMP, PfMP

Hagit Landman, MBA, PMI-SP, PMP

Vanina Mangano, PMI-RMP, PMP

Yvan Petit, PhD, MEng, MBA, PMP, PfMP

Carolina Gabriela Spindola, MBA, SSBB, PMP

X2.2.4 CONSENSUS BODY REVIEW

The following individuals served as members of the PMI Standards Program Consensus Body:

Nigel Blampied, PE, PMP
Chris Cartwright, MPM, PMP
John Dettbarn, DSc, PE
Charles Follin, PMP
Michael Frenette, SMC, PMP
Dana Goulston, PMP
Brian Grafsgaard, PMP, PgMP
Dave Gunner, PMP
Dorothy Kangas, MS, PMP
Thomas Kurihara
Hagit Landman, PMI-SP, PMP
Timothy A. MacFadyen, MBA, PMP

Vanina Mangano, PMI-RMP, PMP
Mike Mosley, PE, PMP
Nanette Patton, MSBA, PMP
Yvan Petit, PhD, PMP
Crispin ("Kik") Piney, PgMP, PfMP
Mike Reed, PMP, PfMP
David Ross, PMP, PgMP
Paul Shaltry, PMP
C. Gabriela Spindola
Chris Stevens, PhD
Judi Vincent
David J. Violette, MPM, PMP

X2.2.5 PRODUCTION STAFF

Special mention is due to the following employees of PMI:

Linda R. Garber, Product Specialist, Publications
Kim Shinners, Product Coordinator, Publications
Barbara Walsh, Product Manager, Publications

X2.2.6 HARMONIZATION TEAM

Core Team:

Bridget Fleming
Greg Hart
Hagit Landman, PMI-SP, PMP
Vanina Mangano, PMP-RMP, PMP
Tim MacFadyen, MBA, PMP
Mike Mosley

John Post, PMP
David W. Ross, PMP, PgMP
Cindy Charlene Shelton, PMI-ACP, PMP
Gary Sikma, PMI-ACP, PMP
Dave Violette, MPM, PMP

PMI Staff:

M. Elaine Lazar, MA, AStd
Marvin R. Nelson, MBA, SCPM
Danielle Ritter, MLIS, CSPO
Lorna Scheel, MSc

Roberta Storer
Kristin Vitello, CAPM
John Zlockie, MBA, PMP

APPENDIX X3
CASE STUDY: BUILDING A CUSTOM BICYCLE

A project building a bicycle was selected to effectively contrast and demonstrate the many estimation practices used in portfolio, program, and project execution. For simplicity, material costs are excluded from this example.

SECTION 2—CONCEPTS

This case study is intended to exemplify estimation development during the project life cycle. It will illustrate iterative estimation, discussing the concepts presented in each section and accompanied by examples (see Figure X3-1). We use a bicycle as an example because it (a) is well understood by populations around the globe, (b) is a relatively simple mechanical model, and (c) has sufficient pieces and parts.

The ACME Bicycle Shop accepts the work to build an ultralight custom bicycle for a cyclist who has a competition in six months and intends to apply for a patent for some unique design features.

For this project, the technical team in the shop must define the design and build a prototype to be tested by the cyclist. Once the cyclist is happy with the prototype, the construction of her bicycle will start. The success criteria of this project are to get the final product delivered to the cyclist in plenty of time to test and tune the bicycle. The cyclist estimates they need to schedule at least two weeks for live road testing.

There are some assumptions and constraints to qualify for this competition:

◆ The bicycle has specifications that limit the weight of the final product, requiring the use of ultralight materials to reach the maximum speed.

◆ At the beginning of the project, it is not clear if the wheels will be manufactured in the store or if they will be purchased.

◆ The cyclist has a prototype crankset that is still in the design phase.

- The work team is not yet formed, but the owner has commitments from two expert colleagues who made special bikes for high-performance competitions a few years ago to come onto the team full-time. The owner knows that these experts will be glad to share their previous experience for estimating and building the new bicycle for the opportunity to work on a cutting-edge designed crankset.

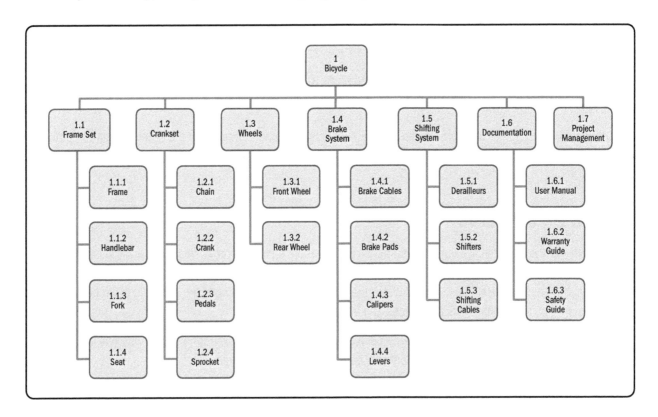

Figure X3-1. Architectural Breakdown of the Project for Building a Custom Bicycle

SECTION 3—PREPARE TO ESTIMATE

The team is gathered to prepare the estimation of the special bicycle for the competition. Their goals are to:

- Validate or, if not available, create a product-oriented WBS;
- Define the estimating approach; and
- Perform a resource gap analysis.

The owner of the store, who is the one who best understands the needs of the cyclist and documents the scope at a high level, has identified a list of activities to be carried out to build the bicycle, and has started an assumption log containing any assumptions and constraints on the project.

Since the project team has been given a WBS, the team asks the cyclist and store owner questions and decides on at least two estimating approaches to enhance the likelihood of developing reliable estimates. The constraints and assumptions are clear and listed in the log.

The project team consults with the stakeholders to gather information required for the Prepare to Estimate stage.

Most of the scope is easy to understand, but the crankset is still being engineered. Because the crankset is still in design, the scope isn't defined enough to estimate the materials and time to machine. The project team decides to split into three smaller teams: teams Alpha, Bravo, and Charlie. Teams Alpha and Bravo will apply different estimating techniques to the same work breakdowns, while team Charlie will use relative estimating techniques to remain adaptable to changes that may need to be made to the crankset.

One of the experts suggests using an analogous estimate, based on his own experience building several bicycles similar to this one a few years ago (minus the crankset). He will lead team Alpha. The second expert chose to contrast that with a bottom-up estimate by estimating component by component up front—she will lead team Bravo, using PERT estimation. Finally, team Charlie is left to work with the owner, machinist, and engineers to iteratively develop the crankset components and use relative estimation. The project team will use three methods to estimate within the project.

SECTION 4—CREATE ESTIMATES

Team Alpha, led by the expert who has built custom models like this one, pulls the historical information on three of those projects for comparison. Comparing the data provided by the expert and normalizing where there are differences, team Alpha agrees on the work breakdown and estimates shown in Table X3-1. In addition, during the review of lessons learned on one of the projects selected for comparison, team Alpha realizes the quality of the braking system purchased commercially off the shelf is equal to the quality of the custom-engineered system originally required. With permission from the owner, they revise the estimates to use commercially procured braking systems and share the change with the entire team.

The project team uses the predetermined approach to Create Estimates for the project using information from similar projects and expert judgment.

Braking systems are available commercially of equal quality and would save the team 20 days for less than half the cost of machining them in-house. The 20 days are derived from the analogous estimate of previously completed work. For team Bravo, the bottom-up estimate needs the following inputs: the WBS shown above (see Table X3-1), the assumptions and constraints already known, and the estimating team.

Table X3-1. Work Packages

Work Package	Duration in Days	Cost in USD
Build Frame Set		
Frame	5	30
Handlebar	4	25
Fork	4	80
Seat	10	100
Build Crankset		
Chain	4	12
Crank	4	10
Pedals	4	23
Sprocket	4	5
Build Wheels		
Front wheel	25	30
Rear wheel	25	30
Build Braking System		
Brake cables	.5	10
Brake pads	1	10
Calipers	.5	5
Levers	1	5
Build Shifting System		
Derailleurs	5	5
Shifters	5	6
Shifting cables	5	8
Create Documentation		
User Manual	20	5
Warranty Guide	10	5
Safety Guide	20	5
Project Management	**20**	**100**

The bottom-up technique actually starts at the highest level and decomposes, considering the bicycle as the deliverable to account for any changes that may have occurred from the WBS creation. Team Bravo uses a product-oriented WBS presenting a predictive life cycle. The decomposition made will produce the estimates at the component level, considering work package deliverables. The outcome is the predicted duration in days and the cost in U.S. dollars. This outcome is intended to be revisited during the life cycle of the project.

Starting with the frame set, the team decomposes the frame into work activities. The project manager decides to use the PERT formula for estimating and asks the team members to prepare three estimates. The first estimate is a best guess, which is the average amount of work the task might take if the team performed the task many times. The second estimate is the pessimistic estimate, which is the amount of work the task might take if the negative factors they identified on the risk log occurred. The third estimate is the optimistic estimate, which is the amount of work the task might take if the positive risks they identified do occur. The team creates three estimates for each work activity for the frame set as shown in Table X3-2.

Table X3-2. PERT Point Estimation—Team Estimates

Activity	Pessimistic (P) Days	Most Likely (ML) Days	Optimistic (O) Days	Result
Tune the computer numerical control (CNC) with the frame CAD drawings	4	3	1	2.8
Create a prototype frame using plastic stock	7	5	2	4.8
Test the tolerances of the prototype	11	8	6	8.2
Create the frame on the CNC	8	5	4	5.3
Test tolerances with other parts	4	3	2	3
Document the settings and adjust drawings to match actual build	2	1	1	1.2
Total Frame Time	**36**	**25**	**16**	**25.3**

Lastly, the team applies a PERT formula (O+4ML+P)/6 to finalize the estimates for the frame set. Using this technique, the team continues estimating the entire WBS as shown in Table X3-3.

Table X3-3. PERT Estimation—Outcome

Work Package	Duration in Days	Cost in USD	Resources
Build Frame Set			
Frame	25	30	Majdi
Handlebar	4	25	Majdi
Fork	4	80	Biyi
Seat	10	100	Biyi
Build Crankset			
Chain	4	12	Cindy
Crank	4	10	Ashley
Pedals	4	23	Cindy
Sprocket	4	5	Ashley
Build Wheels			
Front wheel	25	30	Richard
Rear wheel	25	30	Richard
Build Braking System			
Brake cables	7	10	Paula
Brake pads	7	10	Paula
Calipers	7	5	Paula
Levers	7	5	Biyi
Build Shifting System			
Derailleurs	5	5	Gerhard
Shifters	5	6	Gerhard
Shifting cables	5	8	Gerhard
Create Documentation			
User Manual	20	5	Richard
Warranty Guide	10	5	Linda
Safety Guide	20	5	Linda
Project Management	20	100	Cindy

For team Charlie using an adaptive life cycle, the estimating process is completely different. The team is self-directed to deliver the crankset in time for testing the prototype. Starting from the original WBS, they decompose the crankset into user stories. Here a backlog is created from the WBS using a user story format, so the outcome and limitations are clear and embedded in the work. The user stories replace the documentation the other teams are estimating.

Team Charlie chooses to relatively size the backlog using a nonnumerical scale as an estimation method. From experience the team knows that machining a wheel is a medium-level effort compared to other work. The team selects T-shirt sizing as the relative measure (e.g., Small, Large, and X-Large). Walking through the backlog, the team compares each user story to the known work of a wheel and documents the relative size. The cyclist reminds team members that the minimum viable product of the project is a prototype for her to test.

The project team decomposes the WBS element crankset into user stories and prioritizes the backlog based on experience.

Note: The backlog of user stories must be prioritized before it is input into a schedule. Teams often prioritize the backlog immediately after sizing.

Team Charlie's backlog and estimate are shown in Table X3-4.

Team Charlie decides to build a prototype that can be tested on an existing custom bicycle and prioritizes the backlog according to priority of need to meet the minimum viable product: a prototype bicycle.

The cyclist will be part of the production team working on the design and testing the prototypes. She will provide feedback in order to evolve the prototype and clarify the acceptance criteria.

Teams Alpha, Bravo, and Charlie come together to share their preliminary estimates to develop a rough schedule. They adopt team Charlie's idea of using an existing custom bicycle to test the crankset.

Finally, since a wheel build was the baseline and its estimate was determined to be three days, the crankset was compared to that estimate and normalized to fit into the non-agile portions of the project.

The entire team adopts an agile practice of using information radiators or Kanban charts, and avoids the development of a Gantt chart. Using daily standups and practices to track the completed work in the information radiator as it is completed, the project manager can easily monitor progress and share important knowledge with the rest of the team. The team was given an order-of-magnitude estimate of US$500 for the total effort. Commercial part estimates were provided from a catalog.

Working around schedules and parts lead times, the entire team consolidated the various estimates for each work package and created the overall project estimation baseline (see Table X3-4).

WBS Element	User Story	Size (relative)
Crankset	As a cyclist, I need a crankset that will deliver a ratio of <secret >* so that I maximize my effort for grade >20%.	L
Crankset	As a cyclist, I need to create a prototype of the crankset within 30 days so that it may be performance tested with sufficient time to redesign if necessary.	XL
Chain	As a cyclist, the chain on my crankset must withstand a compression of 500-foot pounds so that my crankset can endure 20% grades for over 40 miles in two days.	S
Crank	As a cyclist, the crank of my crankset must be lightweight to decrease the weight of my cycle without compromising strength so I decrease the weight of the cycle by 10%.	S
Crank	As a cyclist, the crank of my crankset must withstand 300-feet/pounds of pressure on the downward stroke continuously over 400 hours so that the reliability exceeds the costs of replacement.	S
Crank	As a cyclist, the crank of my crankset must be serially identified so that it is not confused with other similar crankshafts that use different engineering.	S
Crank	As a cyclist, the crank of my crankset must accept commercial off-the-shelf pedals and not require a custom pedal.	S
Pedals	As the parts manager, I need five days lead time to order the pedals so that they will be here in time for testing.	L
Pedals	As a cyclist, I need my pedals to be interchangeable with any cycle and not customized to this cycle.	XS
Sprocket	As a machinist, I need the crankset computer-aided design (CAD) files so that I can tune the computer numerical control (CNC) machine.	L
Sprocket	As a cyclist, the sprocket of my crankset must meet the custom engineering designs delivered by the owner, using preordered composites that are already available for additive or subtractive manufacturing so that my design remains closely held.	XL
Sprocket	As a machinist, the sprocket of my crankset must use the CNC machine and three-dimensional printer in the machine shop so that I do not have to wait on machine availability.	S

The estimates from teams Alpha and Bravo are very close in most areas, lending a high probability of accuracy in those estimates, except for the bicycle seat. Team Alpha's estimate was based on the materials currently available in the warehouse. Team Bravo's estimate was based on the specifications provided by the cyclist. The cyclist listened to the arguments and decided to stick with her specifications. The project manager updated the assumption log and project documents to reflect the cyclist's decision.

The final estimates are a combination of all the team estimates and are used to create a project baseline schedule (Table X3-5). New activities may be identified in any iteration.

Table X3-5. Bicycle Team Estimate Baseline

Work Package	Duration in Days	Cost in USD	Resources
Build Frame Set			
Frame	2	1,000	Majdi
Handlebar	1	500	Majdi
Fork	.5	250	Biyi
Seat	.5	250	Biyi
Build Crankset			
Chain	–	69	Cindy
Crank	1	500	Ashley
Pedals	–	75	Cindy
Sprocket	8	4,000	Ashley
Build Wheels			
Front wheel	3	1,500	Richard
Rear wheel	3	1,500	Richard
Braking System	–	175	Parts
Build Shifting System			
Derailleurs	6	3,000	Gerhard
Shifters	.5	250	Gerhard
Shifting cables	–	40	Parts
Create Documentation			
Engineering specification update for patent	1	500	Richard
Project Management	14	2,000	Cindy

SECTION 5—MANAGE ESTIMATES

Construction has started and the bicycle is in progress. The information radiators on the team's progress indicate progress according to plan and all parts have been received in the warehouse.

During the first month of work, the cyclist receives additional funding on condition of painting the sponsor's brand on the cyclist's outfit. This will allow acquiring a lighter frame set than the one already acquired. The prototype frame has already been built and the cyclist requires the change.

During a project review, the team comments on the new sponsor change and decides that a reestimate session will be performed to manage these changes. The revised estimation will constitute a new baseline including the approved change.

SECTION 6—IMPROVE ESTIMATING PROCESS

While building the custom cycle, the team conducted several retrospectives to determine if there were any lessons learned for process improvements as well as the root causes of estimation variances. The shop owner's decision to replace the planned custom frame with a commercially available frame decreased time from the schedule. The estimates were changed to also account for lead time to procure the parts as well as estimates for tasks associated with buying versus building.

Because the initial analogous estimates were so close to the three-point estimates, the shop owner realized that the analogous estimate was reliable, and additional efforts involved in three-point estimation did not provide additional confidence.

The team also enjoyed the fun of using T-shirts to size the effort but found them hard to integrate into the overall project estimate. However, the use of a relative item such as T-shirts saved a significant amount of time, which was applied to the task of physically building the bicycle. The team decided to continue the practice with the knowledge that a relative size was worth the challenges with creating an overall project estimate.

APPENDIX X4
ESTIMATING TOOLS AND TECHNIQUES

X4.1 OVERVIEW

While estimating activity resources, activity durations, project benefits (value), and project costs, a myriad of tools and techniques are available for selection by the project team. The assembled list is not comprehensive and many variants exist. For estimating categories, refer to Table X4-1 and for estimating tools and techniques, refer to Table X4-2.

Table X4-1. Estimating Categories

Estimation Category	Description
Quantitative	This technique can only be used when every detail about the project is available.
	This is a time-consuming and costly technique but it provides the most reliable and accurate result. Some tasks are common and frequent so a lot of data are available. Statistical (parametric) models are a set of related mathematical equations in which alternative scenarios are defined by changing the assumed values of a set of fixed coefficients (parameters).
Qualitative	Subjective judgment based on unquantifiable information. Often, qualitative estimates are done with a few cases and are supposed to provide insights into estimation problems.
Relative estimation	Rough order of magnitude or comparative techniques are employed and progressively elaborated until a more accurate estimate or technique is applied.

Table X4-2. Estimating Tools and Techniques

Tool/Technique	Description	Quantitative	Relative	Qualitative
Decomposition	Decomposition is a top-down estimation technique that tries to make a granular list of initially planned tasks. The more granular the tasks associated with a certain requirement in a work breakdown structure (WBS), the closer the planned effort is with its final value, thereby reducing the mean relative error and possible slippage in project deliverables.	X		
Partial decomposition	This approach starts by building a traditional WBS; using progressive elaboration allows it to be taken down a level or two. At that point, the different work components are estimated using a best guess or one of the other estimating techniques listed here.	X	X	
Phased estimation	Phased estimates are common in very large projects utilizing rolling wave techniques. In phased estimates, the near-term estimates are estimated with a high degree of accuracy (+ or − 5%), whereas future estimates may be estimated plus or minus 35%–50%. The estimation accuracy/variance is often established within the organization's governance for consistency.	X	X	X
Delphi, brainstorming, expert judgment	Using experts, estimation based on the brainstorming of one or more experts who have experience with similar projects; a consensus mechanism then produces the estimate. These techniques may be used in different categories.	X	X	X
Statistical data	Taking variables from similar projects and applying the variables to the current project. For example, the cost of concrete per cubic meter in a previous project is used to calculate the concrete requirement for the current project. The concrete requirement for the new project is multiplied by the cost obtained from the previous project. This will provide the total cost of concrete for the current project.	X		

(continued)

Tool/Technique	Description	Quantitative	Relative	Qualitative
Published rates	Industry sources publish parametric estimating data, using published rates that are available. If there is a need to estimate the cost of building a high-rise office building, an estimator may consult an estimating publication and find that the cost of building a six-story, pre-stressed concrete building with a luxurious finish for the offices, plus many other specifications, would be US$175 per square foot. The appropriate rate can be selected and multiplied by the number of square feet for the building being estimated. That would provide the estimated cost.	X		
Ratio	Ratio is like analogy except that there is some basis for comparing work that has similar characteristics but on a larger or smaller scale. For instance, if the effort required to complete a software installation build-out of a 1,550-square-foot restaurant was 1,500 hours, a new restaurant that is 500 square feet could be estimated at an effort of 500 hours.	X	X	
Monte Carlo analysis	A technique that iterates or computes a data point many times, using input values selected at random from probability distributions of possible values, to calculate the distribution of an estimate as a whole.	X		
PERT/three-point	This technique is used to reduce bias and uncertainty in estimation. Instead of finding a single estimate, three estimates are determined and then their average is used as the estimate. An estimate calculated as a weighted average of optimistic (O), pessimistic (P), and most likely outcomes (ML) is as follows: • *Optimistic (O).* Considers the best case and assumes that everything goes better than planned. • *Most Likely (ML).* Considers a normal case and everything goes as usual. • *Pessimistic (P).* Considers the worst case and assumes that almost everything goes wrong. Depending on assessment of the expected distribution of values, two common formulas are: $(O + 4ML + P) / 6 = E$ where E is the estimate (beta distribution/weighted average) or $(O + ML + P) / 3 = E$ (triangular distribution/simple average).	X		

(continued)

Tool/Technique	Description	Quantitative	Relative	Qualitative
Source lines of code (SLOC)	Method of estimating effort to develop an information systems solution based on the projected number of lines of code needed. A disadvantage of this method is that the SLOC count is not available until the coding stage of the software development life cycle has been completed. It is very difficult to express software size in terms of lines of code at the early stages of development. It can be a source for analogous estimation.	X		
Function point analysis	The counting of discrete functions that an information system provides to the user. Function point analysis is a widely cited method for estimating software project size. At the beginning stage of planning, the top-down approach using function point analysis can be applied. Having obtained more systems specifications at later stages, the bottom-up approach might also be used to improve the accuracy of the estimation. However, the bottom-up approach is not a conventional way to use function point analysis.	X		
Regression analysis	This practice tracks two variables to see if they are related. The diagram is then used to create a mathematical formula to use in future parametric estimations.	X		
Story point	User stories are a type of requirement. These are decomposed to a sufficient level for team members to undertake development of the solution. Story points are a relative estimate of the effort required to complete work on a user story and indicates the size of a story relative to a baseline story.			X
Affinity grouping	Team members simply group items together that they agree are like-sized.	X X		X
Use case point	A measure of the relative effort to complete work on a user requirement.	X		X
Ideal days	The number of days of effort that it would take the team to get a story done if the team worked with no interruptions.			X

(continued)

Tool/Technique	Description	Quantitative	Relative	Qualitative
Heuristics	Heuristic is an experience-based technique; it is used when exhaustive estimation based on detailed mathematical formulas is impractical. It is similar to expert judgment, meaning that if the person has done a similar project in the past, then based on heuristics they can provide an estimate along with explanations.	X X		
Rolling wave planning	Technique that uses ongoing progressive elaboration to continually refine an estimate.	X X		X
Range estimation	To increase the reliability and usability of early estimates, the range, not just the most likely value, is included. For example: The project team offers the following range for the cost of a new graphic interface software enhancement: three to eight worker months and US$150,000 to US$320,000. These assume there is a linear relationship between the capacity and cost.	X X		
Planning poker	Planning poker, also called Scrum poker, is a consensus-based, gamified technique for estimating, mostly used to estimate effort or relative size of development goals in software development. Planning poker employs the use of the Fibonacci sequence to assign a point value to a feature or item with the intent to eliminate time as a variable. By eliminating time as the estimate base, the intent is that the team will be less likely to demand more detail and pad estimates. The number is relative size, not time.		X	X
Interviews, surveys, focus groups, observations, and workshops	An approach to elicit information from stakeholders by talking to them directly and/or collections through interviews, surveys, focus groups, observations, and workshops.	X		X
Earned value management (EVM)	Used to determine estimate at completion (EAC) and estimate to complete (ETC).	X X		X
Expert judgment	Judgment provided based upon subject matter expertise.	X		X

GLOSSARY

1. COMMON ACRONYMS

EEF   enterprise environmental factors

EVM   earned value management

OPA   organizational process assets

PERT   Program Evaluation and Review Technique

PMIS   project management information system

WBS   work breakdown structure

2. DEFINITIONS

Accuracy. An assessment of correctness; the closeness of the measurements to a specific value.

Activity Attributes. Multiple attributes associated with each schedule activity that can be included within the activity list. Activity attributes include activity codes, predecessor activities, successor activities, logical relationships, leads and lags, resource requirements, imposed dates, constraints, and assumptions.

Activity Duration. The time in calendar units between the start and finish of a schedule activity. See also *duration*.

Activity Duration Estimate. A quantitative assessment of the likely amount or outcome for the duration of an activity.

Activity List. A documented tabulation of schedule activities that shows the activity description, activity identifier, and a sufficiently detailed scope of work description so project team members understand what work is to be performed.

Adaptive Life Cycle. A project life cycle that is iterative or incremental.

Analogous Estimating. A technique for estimating the duration or cost of an activity or a project using historical data from a similar activity or project.

Anchoring. A bias that occurs when an individual relies too heavily on an initial piece of information in decision making. Anchoring is also the concept of setting an initial estimate (baseline) to measure from.

Baseline. The approved version of a work product that can be changed using formal change control procedures and is used as the basis for comparison to actual results.

Baseline Estimate. A quantitative assessment of the likely amount or outcome for the approved plan for a project.

Basis of Estimates. Supporting documentation outlining the details used in establishing project estimates such as assumptions, constraints, level of detail, ranges, and confidence levels.

Benefits. Estimating or assessing the approximate benefits realizable by implementing the project or program.

Bottom-Up Estimating. A method of estimating project duration or cost by aggregating the estimates of the lower-level components of the work breakdown structure (WBS).

Bottom-Up Estimating Model. A simplified mathematical description of a system or process (used to assist calculations and predictions) that is prepared by starting at the lower, more detailed pieces of work; these estimates are then aggregated into a total quality for the component of work.

Change Control. A process whereby modifications to documents, deliverables, or baselines associated with the project are identified, documented, approved, or rejected.

Change Control Board (CCB). A formally chartered group responsible for reviewing, evaluating, approving, delaying, or rejecting changes to the project, and for recording and communicating such decisions. See also *change control.*

Change Request. A formal proposal to modify a document, deliverable, or baseline.

Communications Management Plan. A component of the project, program, or portfolio management plan that describes how, when, and by whom information will be administered and disseminated.

Confidence Level. A measure of how reliable a statistical result is (expressed as a percentage) that indicates the probability of the result being correct.

Contingency Reserve. Time or money allocated in the schedule or cost baseline for known risks with active response strategies.

Cost Estimate. A quantitative assessment of the likely amount for project, work package, or activity cost.

Create Estimate. This is the stage of estimating activity resources, activity duration, and costs for a project. There are several models and techniques for determining the estimates.

Delphi Method. A systematic, interactive forecasting method that relies on a panel of experts. The experts answer questionnaires in two or more rounds. After each round, a facilitator provides an anonymous summary of the experts' forecasts from the previous round as well as the reasons they provided for their judgments.

Detectability. In the context of risk management, the probability that a risk event's occurrence is capable of being observed (detected).

Determine Budget. The process of aggregating the estimated costs of individual activities or work packages to establish an authorized cost baseline.

Develop Schedule. The process of analyzing activity sequences, durations, resource requirements, and schedule constraints to create the project schedule model for project execution and monitoring and controlling.

Duration. The total number of work periods required to complete an activity or work breakdown structure component, expressed in hours, days, or weeks.

Earned Value Management. A methodology that combines scope, schedule, and resource measurements to assess project performance and progress.

Enterprise Environmental Factors. Conditions, not under the immediate control of the team, that influence, constrain, or direct the project, program, or portfolio.

Estimate. A quantitative assessment of the likely amount or outcome of a variable, such as project costs, resources, effort, and durations.

Estimate Activity Durations. The process of estimating the number of work periods needed to complete individual activities with estimated resources.

Estimate Activity Resources. The process of estimating team resources and the type and quantities of material, equipment, or supplies necessary to perform project work.

Estimate at Completion (EAC). The expected total cost of completing all work expressed as the sum of the actual costs to date and the estimate to complete.

Estimate Costs. The process of developing an approximation of the monetary resources needed to complete project activities.

Estimate to Complete (ETC). The expected cost to finish all the remaining project work.

Estimating Life Cycle. The duration of estimating in a project, which includes the stages of: Prepare Estimate, Create Estimate, Manage Estimate, and Improve Estimating Process.

Forecast. An estimate or prediction of conditions and events in the project's future, based on information and knowledge available at the time of the forecast.

Historical Information. Documents and data on prior projects including project files, records, correspondence, closed contracts, and closed projects.

Identify Risks. The process of identifying individual risks, as well as sources of overall risk, and documenting their characteristics.

Improve Estimating Process. This project estimating stage is used as the project's progress. Lessons learned are applied to the estimating process, which includes calibrating the models based on actual values and maintaining checklists of areas to include in the estimates.

Integrated Change Control. Identifying, documenting, approving or rejecting, and controlling changes to the project baselines in a coordinated manner across all involved disciplines and Knowledge Areas to ensure overall integrity of the final product; includes an assessment of impact to project time, project cost, and project resources.

Kanban Boards. A visualization tool that enables improvements to the flow of work by making bottlenecks and work quantities visible.

Lessons Learned. The knowledge gained during a project which shows how project events were addressed or should be addressed in the future for the purpose of improving future performance.

Manage Estimate. This project estimating stage is used when the original estimate is completed and the project work has started. Many activities are used, including change controls, calibrating the forecast, and comparing actuals to the estimate.

Manage Stakeholder Engagement. The process of communicating and working with stakeholders to meet their needs and expectations, address issues, and foster appropriate stakeholder involvement.

Organizational Process Assets. Plans, processes, policies, procedures, and knowledge bases specific to and used by the performing organization.

Parametric Estimating. An estimating technique in which an algorithm is used to calculate cost or duration based on historical data and project parameters.

Parametric Estimating Model. A simplified mathematical description of a system or process used to assist calculations and predictions. Generally speaking, parametric models calculate the dependent variables of cost and duration on the basis of one or more variables.

Precision. The closeness of two or more measurements to each other.

Precision, Level of. The number of decimal places to which a numerical estimate will be given.

Predictive Life Cycle. A form of project life cycle in which the project scope, time, and cost are determined in the early phases of the life cycle.

Prepare to Estimate. This is the estimating stage that includes the identification of activities, determining the techniques to be used for estimating, identifying the estimating team, preparing estimating inputs, and documenting any constraints to the estimate (e.g., cost, schedule, resources).

Program Evaluation and Review Technique (PERT). A technique used to estimate project duration through a weighted average of optimistic, pessimistic, and most likely activity durations when there is uncertainty with the individual activity estimates.

Progressive Elaboration. The iterative process of increasing the level of detail in a project management plan as greater amounts of information and more accurate estimates become available.

Project Estimating. The act of creating a quantitative and qualitative assessment of the likely amount or outcome. Usually applied to project costs, benefits, resources, effort, and durations.

Project Estimating Approach. A document, created in the Prepare Estimate stage, which outlines the overall approach, techniques used, project information assumptions, constraints, and other important information needed to create the estimates.

Project Life Cycle. The series of phases that a project passes through from its start to its completion.

Project Management Information System (PMIS). An information system consisting of the tools and techniques used to gather, integrate, and disseminate the outputs of project management processes.

Project Schedule. An output of a schedule model that presents linked activities with planned dates, durations, milestones, and resources.

Ratio Estimating. A model that presumes there is a linear relationship between the cost of a project with one (or more) of the basic features of its deliverable. The basic deliverable features that will need to be quantified and used with this model are either physical attributes or performance characteristics.

Relative Estimation. A technique where tasks, user stories, planning packages, or other grouped items of work are compared to an agreed-upon model or grouped by equivalent difficulty. Relative estimation can save significant time and costs by reapplying the time spent to quantify estimates to doing actual work, thereby delivering business value sooner. It is also designed to take advantage of the learning curve by estimating in near real time and/or short durations.

Resource Calendar. A calendar that identifies the working days and shifts upon which each specific resource is available.

Retrospective. A regularly occurring workshop in which participants explore their work and results in order to improve both the process and product.

Risk Register. A repository in which outputs of risk management processes are recorded.

Rough Estimate. Also known as a *ballpark estimate*, this is an inexact representation of something that is still close enough to be useful.

Rough Order of Magnitude (ROM) Estimate. *See rough estimate.*

Schedule Compression. A technique used to shorten the schedule duration without reducing the project scope.

Scrum. An agile framework for developing and sustaining complex products with specific roles, events, and artifacts.

Stakeholder. An individual, group, or organization that may affect, be affected by, or perceive itself to be affected by a decision, activity, or outcome of a project, program, or portfolio.

Standard. A document established by an authority, custom, or general concept as a model or example.

Story Point. A unitless measure used in relative user story estimation techniques.

Templates. A partially complete document in a predefined format that provides a defined structure for collecting, organizing, and presenting information and data.

Three-Point Estimating. A technique used to estimate cost or duration by applying an average or weighted average of optimistic, pessimistic, and most likely estimates when there is uncertainty with the individual activity estimates.

Variance Analysis. A technique for determining the cause and degree of difference between the baseline and actual performance.

Velocity. A metric that predicts the amount of work an adaptive team can accomplish during an iteration, based upon reflecting on and measuring the work done in previous iterations. This is typically measured in relative terms, such as story points, developer points, user stories, requirements, etc., completed. It allows the team to plan its next capacity more accurately by looking at its historical performance (yesterday's weather). Teams might discover it can take four to eight iterations to achieve a stable velocity.

Work Breakdown Structure (WBS). A hierarchical decomposition of the total scope of work to be carried out by the project team to accomplish the project objectives and create the required deliverables.

Work Performance Information. The performance data collected from controlling processes that are analyzed in comparison with project management plan components, project documents, and other work performance information.

INDEX